INSIGHTS ON THE JOURNEY

TRAUMA, HEALING
AN ANTHOLOGY OF

Compiled and edited by ___ Leach, OSF

ACKNOWLEDGEMENTS

Special thanks to all the women who have shared their stories:
sharing what they have learned
on their own journey from trauma to healing,
and serving as midwives of healing and wholeness for others.

Thanks to Naomi Shihab Nye for permission to use
"You Have to be Careful" and "Gate A-4" ©2007

Thanks to all who served as proofreaders

Cover Photo by Maureen Leach, OSF taken at
Lancetilla Botanical Garden, Honduras

Artwork by Nancy Olinger (Unless otherwise credited)
Art consultant: Polly A. Fowler
Book design by Susan Ives

Additional copies of this book and other peaceCENTER eBOOKS
can be downloaded from www.salsa.net/peace/ebooks
The modest amount we charge for these books
funds the work of the peaceCENTER

**Focused on the vision of Peace in our lives,
the interfaith peaceCENTER supports
the learning of peace through prayer and education;
and supports the demonstration of peace through
nonviolent actions and community**
The peaceCENTER is a 501(c)(3) nonprofit organization

peaceCENTER
1443 S. St. Mary's, San Antonio, TX 78210
210-224-HOPE www.salsa.net/peace

Table of Contents

Prologue
By Maureen Leach, OSF

Is there a universal truth about inner healing? Some suggest there are no universal truths: each person's journey to inner healing is unique. And yet there is certain universality to healing.

This book's disclaimer is to claim beyond a shadow of a doubt that this is not an *"if only"* book. This book is not meant to tell the reader, that *"if only"* you follow a certain practice, you will know inner healing. This book is not meant to purport that *"if only"* you tell your story, keep a secret, confront a certain person, forgive someone, help others, put yourself first, stand on one foot and proclaim certain words, meditate more, or go to this or that self-help group that you will know healing. Any of these practices may or may not be helpful for the reader. Any practices the authors share are because they are personally meaningful and are not meant to say that you have to follow the same route, or you don't "really want to be healed."

Because each person's journey is unique, a particular strategy may be helpful to you, or it may remind you of something entirely different that is more helpful, or it may confirm that this is something that doesn't fit for you right now. Some of the sections of this book may sound like the author is giving advice, which is not the goal. For example, in my own writing I am recounting the advice I give to myself or the practices that work for me.

If I tell you that reaching out to others is what gives me life, it may prompt you to take a break from reaching out for a time and find some space for you.

If I let you know that reading enlightens me, you may decide that right now you don't want to hear about anyone else's pain.

If I reveal how healing it is for me to be at a ranch and spend time with the horses there, it may remind you of how much it helps you to sit at home and have your cat cuddle up next to you.

If I convey to you how expressive movement, dancing, drumming, healing music, hiking, or swimming bring me to a deeper level on the healing journey, it may spark your desire to slow down and do nothing to get to a similar place.

If I make it known that a warm bubble bath by candlelight nourishes me, it may lead you to go get a pedicure.

If I rely on a tried and true list of healing activities, you may prefer a more spontaneous approach to discovering life-giving practices.

If I bring to light how beneficial it has been for me to share my story with another human being, you may be at a point in your journey where you need to distract yourself from dwelling on the story.

I may need to remember, and you may need to forget.

The point is that I needed to find what worked for me, and I hope that this book can be instrumental in finding what works for you and in walking in solidarity with others who may do things differently.

I have invited others to be a part of creating this book so that you may benefit from a variety of perspectives. Some use poetry; some use prose. Some will share personal stories, and others will add perspective from their walk with people who were healing from the inside out. One may tell of a dramatic one time experience of healing, while others may tell of a long slow process. Each tells a unique story.

> *Spiritual guidance quotes are interspersed throughout the chapters in quote boxes that include words of Wisdom from a Spiritual Amma, Jean Springer. At first her words were clumped together in one chapter, but it seemed more appropriate to let the messages shed light on various chapters. This way the spiritual guidance is set within the context of the lived experience.*

Affirmations and one-liners are phrases that can be placed on a mirror, the refrigerator, or a post-it note. They can even be useful as a marquee on your screen saver. You can find affirmations hidden in letters from friends. They can remind you of your inner strength and support system at times when stress levels are high. Look for affirmation and one-liner boxes throughout the book.

A part of the journey to inner healing involves sharing with others – not staying alone in the pain – not staying forever in the pain – learning that life is bigger than what we have suffered.

Knowing, naming, and feeling the pain are often important steps along the way.

If after reading this book you want to write your own chapter, I would love to hear from you. Send your response to: pcebooks@yahoo.com.

Chapter 1
Boundaries, Secrets, and Truth Telling
By Maureen Leach, OSF

You Have to be Careful

You have to be careful telling things.
Some ears are like tunnels.
Your words will go in and get lost in the dark.
Some ears are flat pans like the miners used looking for gold.
What you say will be washed out with the stones.

You look a long time till you find the right ears.
Till then, there are birds and lamps to be spoken to,
a patient cloth rubbing shine in circles,
and the slow, gradually growing possibility
that when you find such ears,
they already know.

Naomi Shihab Nye, © 2007

I first heard this poem at a workshop on working with trauma survivors. It speaks so clearly of the dynamics between secrets and truth telling. Who has not known the pain of sharing something that was not well received? Finding the right ears is a lonely search. Traumas or hearing about traumas trigger extreme responses in people. The tendency of many survivors is to tell no one about a trauma or to tell everyone. Finding the right ears is a process of establishing effective boundaries. How do I create a boundary that works? It needs to be something less stern than the Berlin Wall, something safer than a leaky dike in Holland, something less transparent and more permeable than the glass sides of an aquarium; something that will allow me to enter space with another — without being trampled.

> *The first step is to befriend our lives, befriend our bodies.*

What would it be like if there were no rules about what could be said? What would it be like if I didn't have to keep secrets in order to protect people? What would I say if I were totally free to say whatever I wanted and I knew that whatever I said would be heard by the right ears? What if I knew it was safe to say what was longing to be said in the depth of my being?

Maybe you have someone in your life that has the right ears. If you have not yet found that person, you may consider writing your story. You may trust yourself to be those ears as you put pen to paper to tell your story. If it is right for you, start a healing journal.

You could include:

- ❖ What you would say if you could say anything and know only the right ears would hear
- ❖ A list of things that help if you are having a hard day
- ❖ A list of resources available to you
- ❖ Fun things to do when life gets heavy and you need a break from the inner work
- ❖ A list of people that you can call upon for support
- ❖ Ways people have helped you on the journey
- ❖ Quotes from books, songs, or people that have helped you on the journey
- ❖ Poems
- ❖ Affirmations
- ❖ Dreams
- ❖ Techniques for dealing with triggers - things that work for you, helping ground you in the present
- ❖ Signs of progress or growth to lift your spirit when you are feeling down
- ❖ Reflections on what is being born in you

On Birth:

Birth is such a simple story –
One that happens
within the lives of each of us.
I have watched a foster parent
give an infant unconditional love.
I have listened
to a husband faithfully birth his dying wife into Life Eternal.
I have seen a sparkle in the eyes of a grandmother
as she spoke of the birth of her newborn grandchild.
I have seen lights of hope in people as they faced fear or loss
or confusion or illness.

Words of Wisdom from a Spiritual Amma – Jean Springer

Slow Down

Inner healing happens slowly. People often feel an urgency to have complete and total healing and have it quickly. Yet, more often than not, the process is slow.

People have told me what inner healing is supposed to be like, and I have tried to pretend I had arrived without going through the work to get there. In the model that people described, forgiveness was the ultimate goal. But that formula doesn't work for me. In fact, putting the goal as forgiveness may not be the way to go at all. Perhaps premature forgiveness is merely an acceptable name for denial.

> *Perhaps premature forgiveness is merely an acceptable name for denial.*

Setting the right pace is important in the healing process. There needs to be a balance. Too much focus on the trauma leaves me wallowing in pain. Inadequate focus causes me to bury feelings that will explode later.

I have an 8 ½ by 11 sign that says SLOW DOWN. It was created for a conference where I was serving as a simultaneous Spanish/ English language interpreter. The purpose of the sign was for the interpreters to inform the speakers that we needed time to catch up with what they were saying. Years after the conference the sign still serves as a useful reminder to me during my own life's journey. It says:

Slow down, my friend.

Take time to notice the present moment
and what it holds for you.

Take time to notice what is beautiful around you.

Slow down and taste the food and savor the goodness.

Take time to believe in yourself.

Take time to tell your friends how much they mean to you.

Take time for quiet;
let your inner spirit connect with your Source.

Take time to be grateful for what is going well.

If things seem to be in a state of turmoil,
take time to remember when things were better.

If you are really lonely,
take time to remember sacred moments shared with friends.

If you are feeling miserable,
take time to acknowledge that feelings don't last forever.

If you are feeling powerless, respect the place where you are,
and when it is time move to your place of inner strength.

If you are feeling afraid, name your fear,
let go of any blame associated with it,
search your memory, and tap into a space where you felt safe.

If you are feeling frustration, anger, or rage – notice the emotion,
decide what you need it for, and when it no longer serves you
let it go.

If you are feeling anything, celebrate the ability to feel.

If you are numb,
know that it is the body's way of telling you to slow down.

If you are dealing with
grief, trauma, or intense feelings of any kind:
slow down.

Slow down enough for your dreams to awaken in you.

*Know my love
surrounds you and
my belief in you
is unbounded*

Learning and Unlearning
By Maureen Leach, OSF

Life is a constant flow of learning and unlearning. I learn things that serve me for a time and then there comes a time to let go and move on.

There may be rules I learned about how to keep safe that work perfectly well for a time and then one day they get in the way.

Take the analogy of a car. Basic safety tells me to get in and buckle up. Added safety measures may include locking the doors and having the windows up. Yet, in August 2007 when a bridge collapsed in Minneapolis, all new rules came into play. The news reports said that on a bridge that is about to collapse, everything is turned around. Then safety requires that the seat belt be unbuckled, the doors unlocked and the windows down.

> *I make mistakes and I try again.*
> *I have a sense of humor*
> *and I can laugh,*
> *but I don't laugh so much*
> *that I forget to go deeper.*

It is important to me not to be rigid about following what worked in the past and to be open to what the present moment requires. This is where discernment enters.

When I was in Guatemala, I suffered from severe diarrhea caused by amoebas. I was given medicine that caused gastritis. I was instructed to avoid fresh fruits and vegetables that may have been washed in contaminated water and to avoid spicy foods that would irritate the gastritis.

When I returned to the United States, it took me a long time to let go of those rules. I could walk into a grocery store and go up and down the aisles for over an hour and leave with less than $10 worth of groceries. Rules upon rules seemed to be paralyzing me. One person said not to eat any sugar, that it would cause depression. So, a rule against eating sugar was created and added to the rule against fresh fruit and vegetables that was added to the rule against eating spicy foods. And then there was the rule of trying to live simply in spite of the exhorbitant cost of things in the United States. Those rules piled on top of rules were overwhelming. I came to think of food itself as being unhealthy. If I ate, I got sick, and of course it was my fault for not guessing the right thing to eat. I had this terrible habit of blaming myself for everything that went wrong.

One day, a wise woman taught me to put those rules aside and know that I could bring them back out again if I returned to Guatemala. She declared that I could eat whatever I wanted and I would not get sick. When I doubted her, she said that if I did get sick it would be her fault and not mine. Sure enough it worked. I started eating and gaining back some of the weight I had lost, and I learned to trust myself again.

It wasn't until years later that I began to work with the Federation of Returned Overseas Missioners that I realized that many missioners experience trauma going into a grocery store and are overwhelmed with the number of choices and the cost of things. I learned that it was a common experience for those returning to feel paralyzed in a grocery store. The lesson was that sharing with others made me feel much less isolated and able to have a sense of solidarity with others who return after living in other countries.

I heard other missionaries discredit their own experiences of trauma because others had it so much worse. It was clear that each of their experiences counted no matter how short or long they were. Yet, it took a long time for me to have that same compassion for myself. I heard people saying, "You should be over the grief by now, you were only there 2 years." I added my own voice of judgment saying, "You were not the one who was kidnapped and tortured, why are you experiencing so much trauma?"

> *On Change:*
> *We are constantly asked to stretch*
> *beyond our self-imposed limitations and*
> *embrace a wider perspective, a deeper possibility.*
> *I see in the lives of people I meet, a unique unfolding of their*
> *lives and their direction through the responses they make to*
> *what life asks of them.*
>
> Words of Wisdom
> from a Spiritual Amma – Jean Springer

I learned to ignore the inner and outer voices that were judgmental and allowed the grief to have its own timetable. When it was time, I let go, and the following poem speaks of the process.

Rules Long Past and Fears by the Wayside

Black on yellow
    Glaring me in the face
"Watch for ice on the bridge"

     I need to be very careful
I know what it is like ...
To be rear ended in an ice storm . . .

   Protect yourself,
     Caution,
       Beware,
         Jach tel cu taj,
           ja wil ha pa,
             ten cuidado,
              be on guard

   The message comes
in every language that has been a part of me.
    WAIT!
It is the time when wild flowers
Are about to bloom.

It is over 80 degrees outside.
Fold up that sign, I don't need it today
Save the fears for a cold wet winter day.
'Tis spring and fear of ice serves me not.

Maureen Leach, OSF
What was done in the past is long past, and things are different now.

I mentally fold up the "Watch for Ice on Bridge" sign and with it the fears - countless fears that are past their time. Without that bright yellow and black sign, I can be bold in new ways.

Yet, signs speak once again. In northern San Antonio on Bitters Road, there is a sign that says "Operation Slow Down." It is accompanied with a sign that proclaims my speed as I drive by. It wouldn't hurt me to reflect on that sign every day. How fast am I going today? How willing am I to participate in "Operation Slow Down"?

How willing am I to "Drive Friendly" in this world of ours? "Drive Friendly" seems to be a sign that is unique to Texas. It means to move over to the shoulder so that those who want to go faster can pass. Paying attention to "Drive Friendly" signs tells me to set my own pace and not to expect others to go at my pace or to judge myself according to the pace of others.

Another famous Texas sign is "Don't slow Texas down", which seems to mean that if you are going the speed limit or less, you should stay in the right lane. Sometimes even doing that does not prevent drivers from tailgating and flashing their lights. If I notice someone too close on my tail, I often turn on my 4 way flashers. This is my way of announcing to the world that I need a little space.

Balance knows when to pay attention to the signs that say: "Drive Friendly" and "Don't slow Texas down" and when to focus on: "Operation Slow Down" and "Watch for Ice on the Bridge." Balance knows when to let go and move on and when to step back and proceed with caution. Balance finds its own rhythm of holding on and letting go.

I am so glad that you follow your heart and soul, even when it takes you into entirely new directions.

A True Story That Really Happened
Holding On and Letting Go –

We built a fence
A fence to keep the chickens in
We couldn't go deep
The rocks would not let us
The raccoon took advantage
Of our shallow walls
In he came and killed the chicken and
Maimed Ricardo, the rooster

Aye, Ricardo, will you ever feel safe again?
The raccoon is dead
The death penalty he received
Shot three times for his terrible deed
But death of a raccoon will not make Ricardo feel
safe again
I feel no sorrow for the raccoon
I never met
I only know compassion for the
one eyed rooster I tenderly hold
Me, a Franciscan,
serving whiskey to a rooster
A rooster who could not feel safe
But, who let me hold him –
Until safe I felt
Safe – holding another's pain
While letting go of my own.

Maureen Leach, OSF

Chapter 2
Poetry and Healing

Then I Met Winter:
By Polly A. Fowler

In the spring of 1999, I began a journey not of my choosing. I was diagnosed with breast cancer. It's not easy to give voice to all that impacts us emotionally and spiritually when faced with situations that unfold so suddenly and traumatically in our lives. But a voice did cry out. In the deepest part of my soul, I knew there was a wounded spirit that begged to be heard, a soul that sought respite and peace, even as my body sought healing. Had the diagnosis not been cancer, these words might have remained forever silent, unspoken; for I never would have chosen to walk this path. I never would have descended into the depths of self long enough to hear the cries of that wounded spirit. "Allegory" is but a whisper of a long forgotten voice.

I'm Not at Peace with the Unfolding
A January Allegory

I am not at peace with the unfolding,
the twists and turns of the pathway
that leads through forests with branches that hang low
and catch my body and shape my path
and frighten me . . .

I see the dancing of the light and the dark, and the play of shadows
in the mist.
I don't know what's out there.
I trip often
and fall
flat on my face,
flat on my face, as they say.

I hide my face in the mud and the muck.
(Perhaps someone is telling me to be one with the earth.)

And on my face I feel the wet, wet leaves that once were trimmed
in gold.
Who took away the gold? Was it the rain? Or my tears? … or fears?
Or do I just not see the wisdom of the seasons.
There will be gold again, I think.

Still, the darkness, for all its wisdom, remains as dark.
So, too the mud . . .
I don't know what I'll find here in this forest
where darkness beckons me
and branches catch my body
and shape my path . . .

I seem to go from me to me,
From who I am to who I am.
With all my twists and turns
I go full circle and am just as lost.
I am no different now than I was then at the beginning . . .
or was that the end?
Circles go nowhere.
Am I not the same traveler on this same round pathway,
in this same forest,
and these same trees,

and these same branches that catch my body
and ...
Oh, Forget it!
I've just crossed a lot of nowhere bridges,
I've stumbled here before.
And now I'm lost . . . or think I'm lost. It is as frightening.

The maze of trees is forbidding [or is it bidding?]
hiding a terror
What terror? My mind plays tricks with me,
Having me see what there is not to see.
No terror . . .

Let the forest and the darkness lead me.
It is the only path that offers hope
to the child in the mist who can not cry,
to the little boy lost who can not see,
It is the only path.
It is the only path.

How often I have gone from north to south,
from top to bottom, from outside in.
You would think I would know all there is to know of me,
but I don't.
I go back out and north, again, you see.

Yes, you see . . .
Observer,
Judge.
What is it you see?

Whish-sh-sh-sh . . . spirit – wind . . .
I saw it, too,
fleeting.
Was that the same thing you saw – in me?
I so want to hold on to the wind
and let it kiss,
and kiss,
and kiss,
and nurture me.
But I am so frightened by the night,
by its secrets and its shadows.

Wait!
There is a terror here!
Who is it that spies on me?
Who sees me
in this mud and in this muck,
with my face buried in these wet, wet leaves –
these leaves once trimmed in gold?

Who took away the gold?
Was it rain?
Or tears?
Or my ancient, ancient fears?
God! Was it Him, not me?
Oh, if I could but see the wisdom of the seasons,
I would embrace these leaves
And rest my soul upon this earth,
And dream sweet dreams of gold.
There will be gold again, I think.

I'm not at all at peace with this unfolding.
I don't know what there is yet to be . . .
except me.

I hope in gold. I hope in gold.

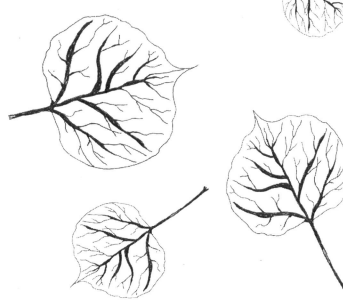

Do not be dismayed

Do not be dismayed by my silence or distance:
the barrier to trust is formidable
    strengthened by pain
    and the renewal of pain.
Reminders renew conflict in that inner sanctum
    where love and hurt reside.
I must flee
    in silence
    or in deed.
I wish I could have allowed your touch to soothe me
    or taken rest
    in the sanctuary of your eyes.

Polly A. Fowler, 1984

Windmill

Tall sentinel,
catcher of an ageless voice,
gentle listening
ear of breezes
 brought by seasons as they come
 and go,
    lend me your strength
    to listen, too,
     to all that speaks within my
     heart.
    to spirit winds
      that in their wisdom
      blow across the seasons
    of my life
     to give my life a soul.

Polly A. Fowler, 1997

October Grace

I'm so glad that grace has pulled you through
      and left the Master's touch upon your eyes
      enough for me to see
That grace was sent through you
      as gift
      for me...

Polly A. Fowler, 1988

Hurting and Healing

Growing Beyond Depression, Withdrawl, and Anxiety Through Relationships and Acceptance

By Catherine Na

Depression

I think I'm dulled inside.
Too much cotton.
Not enough appreciation of
      sharp beauties surrounding,
      poignant moments abounding,
      calls to life astounding.

It's been too much,
the aloneness
and wondering if I'm lost
and constantly feeling not good enough.
(Just where was it I made that disastrous mistake?)
There's too much emptiness here.

Yes, I'm dulled inside.
Maybe I need to sharpen some tools –
eat   sleep   exercise   breathe right,
cook more,
write friends,
nurture relationships,
get realistic at work.

My hand is limp
as I reach for sharpening tools.
It falls back to my lap
and picks up the TV remote again.

Catherine Na

Again

Another wall came banging down firmly in place,
like a garage door jerked shut.
It's just that fast.

Let's see,
how many layers
does that make now?

There's got to be a better
way
to handle getting
hurt
than living
alone inside
a deep, deep
labyrinth
of walls on
garage door tracks.

Catherine Na

Grief has its own timing.

Anxiety on a Rampage

Multiple priorities, time-crunch, living on the edge,
        challenged authority, self-doubts, working in structures that
don't work
have
led
to
anxiety on a rampage:

sleepless 4 a.m.s,
seared stomach,
tightening muscles,
tightening psyche,
tightening words.

Flow, soul; flow!
Let go.
Accept the blows,
the half-successes,
the bitter disappointments.
You will outlive them.
The rain comes.
Listen to its falling, its splashing.
Feel its cooling, its washing.
Let your own gentle care envelope you.

And, for God's sake, go see a comedy!

Catherine Na

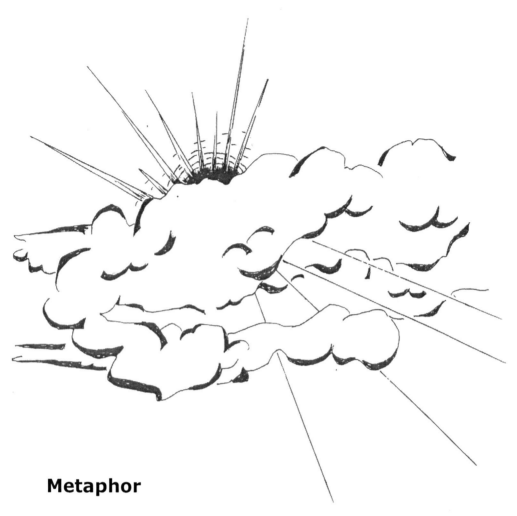

Metaphor

That huge ol' sun
rose
so bright, so powerful
incredible orange-pink light *light* LIGHT,
rising gloriously.

A cloud,
miniscule to the sun
and nothing but vapor,
blocked.

Because, you see,
the cloud was so much closer to me.

Catherine Na

*Here is a poem I wrote during an international meeting of
leaders, in celebration of healing & growth of all kinds.*

What Gets Through

Light pushes in through slat cracks.
Birdsong pierces the traffic din.
Breakfast smells permeate
     rooms behind closed doors,
     down distant hallways.

Desire to comprehend pushes in through language limitations.
Shared human suffering pierces prejudice.
Artists' truths permeate
     diverse cultural settings
     in all parts of the world.

Love pushes in through ignorance.
Humor pierces fatalistic drive .
God-life permeates
     flaccid human history
     in a cosmos of possibilities.

     It's amazing what gets through!

Catherine Na

Dedicated to Gary, the best hugger I know

Real Hug

In a real hug,
the inside shaking
stops;

the uncried tears
find themselves
in a puddle-heart;

and the tumped vials
of inner preciousness
are set upright again.

In a real hug,
a kind darkness
envelopes;

a soft firmness
of strength
stabilizes and centers;

and an unknown future
with hope
is entered.

In a real hug.

Catherine Na

Whenever I think of you, I smile with joy

Like Precious Rain

Like precious rain
your love descends upon me,
soaking my surface,
penetrating my layers,
feeding the roots of my soul.

Your love
urges the life inside me
to blossom.
          It soothes my parchedness
and washes the grit away.
It stills my fluttering
but has me bouncing more
slowly and deeply.

So I enjoy
and smile
and soak in
your precious rain,

and let it change me.

Catherine Na

Another Metaphor

The sun's rising is met by clouds,
  and the clouds by the sun's rising.
     Darkness is given enough light
       for gray to be.
     This is enough light to walk by.

       The rising continues.
       Stronger light shines from behind a filmy
        bank of clouds.
        Rays travel with the wind-blown film,
        mustily illuminating parts of the landscape,
       traveling from hill to hill.

     The rising continues.
    Up from behind that first bank
  but still hidden by other banks,
  the sun casts color;
first sky-red and sky-gold trimming the clouds,
then the greens of earth
  with its tree-covered hills.

The rising continues.
But now it is met by a strong cloud bank,
dark, dense and ominous.

Rise! Light fills above.

Rise! Light surrounds.
And the wind continues to push that cloudbank
out of the way.

  The sun!
  Light fills sky and earth.
        Now I can see detail.
        Now I can Know.

Catherine Na

The poem I wrote the morning after
I learned I have a form of lymphoma that's terminal.

Magnificence

I am in awe
of Magnificence
far beyond my life –

so far beyond
that it includes death
and love that keeps on going –

a Magnificence
that holds me
in this time of pain

and pulls me deep into this moment
and pulls me beyond this moment

and draws me into
what I have never seen.

Catherine Na

Martha K. Grant shares the next two poems as good reminders of the power of art, both visual and written, in helping deal with painful issues. Art has been a part of her own healing over the years.

RE-MEMBERED

Returning to old scabs,
forgotten scars,
wounds, large and small,
that were never kissed
to stop the hurting,
I wrap a memory in a poem,
a painting;
somehow that bandages it,
kisses the wound,
says a prayer over
the healing.

It keeps me from idly ---
        or intentionally ---
            picking at a loose
            itchy corner of it,
            allows a new healing,
             maybe this time
                without
                    scarring.

                        Martha K. Grant

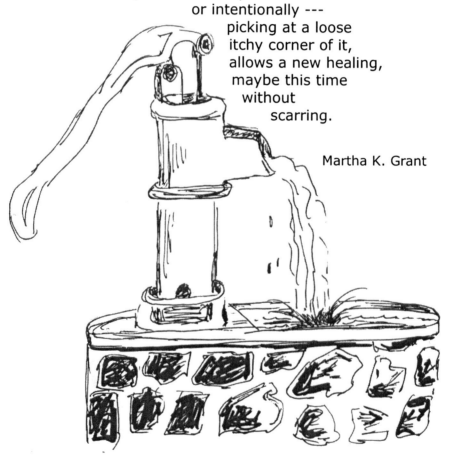

Salvation History

You didn't flinch.
Slowly I read
my poems to you,
line by poignant line,
scanning your face for—
what? What did I
hope to see,
fear to see,
registered there
as I shared
a tentative scrap
of my salvation
history?

You didn't flinch.
Possibly you knew
better than I—
this recounting
of a sordid story
is indeed
my salvation.
With grace
you encouraged it,
with mercy,
received it.

You didn't flinch at
    the telling.
        Someday soon,
        I no longer will.

        Martha K. Grant

Tina Karagulian writes poetry to release emotions surrounding injustice in life and to celebrate the beauty and love she sees within life. One important theme has been the effect of the Armenian genocide on her ancestors and on her own story.

Dark, Velvet Countenance

She calls forth my longing
Her dark, velvet countenance
    illumines
        shields
            exalts,
breaks open the expansive me

I pour forth angelic light
      in all of breath and all of life
          I am warrior in truth

I am mother, defender, creator, lover
      bursting of joys,
         summoning delights

And yet,
  I move beyond all roles
    and ideals in which I am cast:

I simply drink the fullness of my soul

The ultimate Truth is not just
      that She and I are One.

We Ascend Far Beyond *That.*

        Tina Karagulian

Self-Referential

You call me self-referential
Just because I feel much more
Than others do
Just because I go farther than
I choose to go
It's hard to come back
But I always do
You say I always cry
There's nothing new
But sometimes it's not just a release
But a shattering
Can you tell the difference?
Or are you sick and tired
Of my "self-reference"?
I am who I am
I am not perfect
I feel the pulse of the earth
As she breathes in and out
I feel the waves crash
Upon the shores
Even though I am miles away
I feel the separation
That others feel from their God
Does that make me self-referential?
Are my cries
Like the boy who cried wolf?
Are my experiences
Weary travelers
taking up your road?
I experience pain,
But my feelings are anything but fake
My feelings are anything but wrong
All that I feel points to some truth
But if I don't honor my truth
I get flooded
Flooded with emotion
and tears
Until I take time to notice
Until I honor my soul
Until I center myself
So the irony is,
I need more self-reference
To unlock the true me.
                    Tina Karagulian

Transcen*dance*

whose voice can she speak
    in the damp hate
        of genetic expectation ?

in child's cry
    she is denied the milk of life
        in the unnamed abyss
           of soundless cries,

where acts are so violent
    people turn the other cheek
        until she appears extinct—

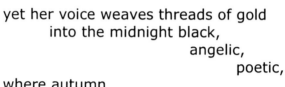

yet her voice weaves threads of gold
    into the midnight black,
        angelic,
          poetic,

where autumn
    drops its colors at her feet,
        and trees bough
        to her soft knowing,

where soil is earthy,
    ready to feed any lack,

where the truth of her
    carries the fullness of ocean
        and her emergence heralds
        infinite promise.

Tina Karagulian

I am glad you were able to let the tears flow.
Sometimes they are the tears that have been stored up for a
long time and something sets them free.
Just let them wash over you and fill
the desert of lives around you.

Words of Wisdom from a Spiritual Amma – Jean Springer

Courted Heart

Vision-dark,
olive soul—
Armenian goddess
inner folds

hold the knowledge
of Genocide past—
release the fight,
the courted heart,
     feminine light,
        shout the spark:

IGNITE,
IGNITE!

Tina Karagulian

Sunburn

for my grandmother

Burned
by the sun
by greed
by circumstances
by religious intolerance
by want of land over people.

Mariam's land,
possessions,
all were taken away,
save for a few gold coins,
swallowed;
in hopes it would
help wherever she landed.
Food gone within days;
Eating desert grass.
When she was with fever,
her husband found meat
to feed her;
he needed her to survive,
he wouldn't tell her what kind of meat
she found out later
it was donkey
lying dead in desert heat.

Her body
felt all of the violence;
bruises made shapes in her skin
violated,
raped and discarded,
by men who could not see her.
The desert sun was not the worst of it
the cold, night chills were not the worst of it.

Going to a new land,
Now a refugee problem,
empty crates for tables,
Working at any odd job
to get food for her family.

But as a mother
losing her three babies
was the worst of it
Seeing mothers' breast milk dry up
and their babies die
was the worst of it
Seeing mothers drown their babies
in the Tigris-Euphrates River
to spare them further torture,
that was the worst of it.
Mothers suffer the most
when they give life
when they nurture life
and violence takes away
what they love most.
Mother Mary understands
Mother Mary knows
Violence has to end sometime.
When?

Tina Karagulian

> *The gift of grief is that people touch us*
> *and create a space within us that*
> *no one else can touch*

Slice of Plenty

"take another helping of abuse while you're at it
      after all, you're strong enough to take it
            it's your job..."

that's what many say,
        many who don't want to see anyone truly happy,
            many who would rather see a pinhole size me
                because any more would blind them

little do they know,
    they have the same glow
        they *can* be reminded
            that sun of their shine can swallow up sky,
               that birds respond in kind to the bird call of humans.

that the moist smell of earth brings hope for all,
        that beating hearts can rhythm down any broken notes
           that you get much more than a slice of plenty

Tina Karagulian

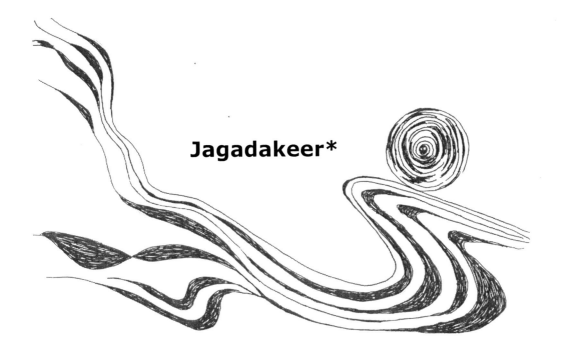

Jagadakeer*

Was it fate that led us through desert sand,
in broken moonlight,
        where whispered dreams floated toward distant stars?

Was it fate that chiseled families into puzzle pieces,
led away "by choice", in a "relocation package"
        complete with all the amenities any genocide can offer?

Was it fate that unanswered prayers remained poised
in cellular memory,
awaiting release only in the presence of true witness?

The poetry of my fate pierces through prisms of soul,
        Triumphant in the language of true ancestry.

Tina Karagulian

*(Jagadakeer is the Armenian word for
"writing on the forehead" or fate.)*

Chapter 3

Lessons from the Ancestors

By Tina Karagulian

When we let go of what we don't need and seek to receive our true calling, we may experience pain in the releasing, but we also receive so much more in return.

I want to tell you a story.

Once there was a woman who lived and worked in the valley between two mountains. She farmed the land with her family, she was strong, and she had one son and three daughters. She went to church every Sunday. One day, she was told to leave her home. Some of her neighbors were being killed. She took whatever possessions she could carry. She left her youngest daughter with a neighbor because she thought her child would be safer there. She and her remaining children, husband, and extended family were forced to walk through the desert. Armed guards would steal whatever gold they would find from those who walked. The sun was very hot during the day, and the nights were very cold. With no shelter, the elements were harsh on the body. Soon there was not enough food or water, and people would die along the way, with no one to give them proper prayers or burials. Young girls were often raped; so many parents would cut their daughters' hair in order to disguise them as boys. The woman who left her daughter with a neighbor heard that the neighbor was *also* forced to walk with them; she searched frantically and miraculously, was able to find her daughter. Her daughter looked angrily at her for leaving her behind; she was too young to understand. Unfortunately, because of the hot sun and lack of food, this daughter contracted a disease and soon died. The woman's two other daughters also died. Finally, this family survived the journey, ending up in a distant country as refugees. Different churches offered food to the refugees if they would become members of those churches. But this woman chose to keep what was left of her identity, which was her church, because her faith is what got her through her ordeal.

This is the story of my maternal grandmother, whom I never met, but whose story I have carried with me.

At one time, half of present-day Turkey was once Armenian land. In 1915, the small, secular and nationalist leadership in Turkey called "The Young Turks" set out to exterminate 1 1/2 million Armenians in the first genocide of that century. In my family, we were lucky that a kind, Turkish man saved my grandfather's life, alerting him in the middle of the night, for he was to be killed in the morning. Yet, even with such kindnesses, approximately 1 1/2 million Armenians were killed. To this day, the governments of Turkey and the United States do not officially recognize that the Armenian Genocide took place.

These stories were truths I learned as a child, that terrible things can happen to your family, to your identity, but that the truth of God and church were stronger.

Growing up, I listened to the beautiful Armenian church music. I found something beautiful amidst the shame and sadness of my culture. The music took me beyond the labels and limiting beliefs that came from the genocide. Then the day came when I asked a question and the speaker made a comment that women could not become Armenian priests. I remember the life being kicked out of me. I realized that although I felt this incredible pull to serve God, those around me could not see it or allow it. Sadly, a young Armenian girl could only go so far within the Armenian Church.

My first internship in college was in a day treatment program for people suffering from mental illness. I didn't know what to expect. I found out that just sitting with others and being fully present with them made a big difference. On the last day of my internship, I said my goodbyes to everyone in the group, and one man spoke up. He often spoke in sentences you did not understand, often "delusional" as others put it. And yet, in that moment, he was very clear, commenting on my sincerity and thanking me for being there. I knew then that I had made a connection, that I was serving God. I was listening to the stories of others, people I did not know or grow up understanding, but I was honoring their soul. I was where God wanted me to be, to understand the suffering of others and see their souls as equal to my own.

God asked me to let go of all the beliefs that limited me; beliefs that I am a victim because of the genocide my culture endured, beliefs that to let my spirit shine is somehow a sin. I prayed to God daily, angry at times, desolate at others. I realize that I often felt God's presence, but most of the time I was too afraid or too angry to let God in.

I asked God to take away all the pain I held onto, from the pain of my life and the pain I carried from my ancestors. Peace and unconditional love would enter my heart, and from that peaceful place, I felt the expansiveness of my soul. For me, part of that process includes honoring my painful experiences as part of who I am, as part of my ministry. I can't just ignore that piece and jump to the peaceful part of the story, however many times I am tempted.

Because of my life experiences, I have seen what happens when a war is considered over. People who are left behind must somehow learn to let go of survival mode and begin to learn to trust people again and to give emotionally to themselves and to their children. How people cope emotionally affects generations to come.

Because of my life experiences, I have seen what happens when some people are not valued as equal members of a village, of a country, of a church. Driving people out to walk in the desert, or driving people from a church community...there is little difference. The effects are devastating to someone's spirit. For that reason, I will always speak out against inequality. Even though it is

> *Because of my life experiences, I have seen what happens when some people are not valued as equal members of a village, of a country, of a church. Driving people out to walk in the desert, or driving people from a church.*

at times difficult for me to do, I have come to learn that this voice of mine is also part of my calling.

Writing this got me in touch with my grandmother's journey in a way I did not anticipate. I felt her losses even deeper than before. I felt the loss of all mothers who see their children suffer, and I prayed about how to heal all the mothers of my ancestors. I entered a place of divine mothering, a place where I do not have to have words. In this space, I do not have to be linear, and I have all the room I need to let go of all the anger and fear from the stories that I have held; when we go into that place within our hearts, we can achieve wholeness again; whatever was lost or stripped from us *can* be restored. This mothering energy is not passive, but strong, protective, and giving, and we deserve to receive it. By receiving, we can begin to see our cup as full and not empty, and celebrate all that we receive and are thankful for.

I am thankful for the strength of my grandmother, for her faith in God, and for what she gave her community after walking through the desert. She was a midwife and offered healing cures for her Armenian neighbors.

I had to renounce a way of life I thought I would have led and a church community I thought I would have served. But look at all that I have received. In the renouncing, we receive so much more in return.

Chapter 4
Healing Connections

Gate A-4
By Naomi Shihab Nye

Wandering around the Albuquerque Airport Terminal, after learning my flight had been detained four hours, I heard an announcement: "If anyone in the vicinity of Gate A-4 understands any Arabic, please come to the gate immediately." Well – one pauses these days. Gate A-4 was my own gate. I went there. An older woman in full traditional Palestinian embroidered dress, just like my grandma wore, was crumpled to the floor, wailing loudly. "Help," said the Flight Service Person. "Talk to her. What is her problem? We told her the flight was going to be late and she did this." I stooped to put my arm around the woman and spoke to her haltingly. "*Shu dow-a, Shu-bid-uck Habibti? Stani schway, Min fadlick, Shu-bit-se-wee?*" The minute she heard any words she knew, however poorly used, she stopped crying. She thought the flight had been cancelled entirely. She needed to be in El Paso for major medical treatment the next day. I said, "You're fine, you'll get there, who is picking you up? Let's call him." We called

her son and I spoke with him in English. I told him I would stay
with his mother till we got on the plane and would ride next to her
– Southwest.

She talked to him. Then we called her other sons just for fun. Then we
called my dad and he and she spoke for a while in Arabic and found
out of course they had ten shared friends. Then I thought just for the
heck of it why not call some Palestinian poets I know and let them
chat with her? This all took up about two hours. She was laughing
a lot by then. Telling about her life, patting my knee, answering
questions. She had pulled a sack of homemade mamool cookies
– little powdered sugar crumbly mounds stuffed with dates and nuts
– out of her bag – and was offering them to all the women at the
gate. To my amazement, not a single woman declined one. It was like
a sacrament. The traveler from Argentina, the mom from California,
the lovely woman from Laredo – we were all covered with the same
powdered sugar. And smiling. There is no better cookie. And then the
airline broke out the free beverages from huge coolers and two little
girls from our flight ran around serving us all apple juice and they were
covered with powdered sugar too. And I noticed my new best friend
– by now we were holding hands – had a potted plant poking out of
her bag, some medicinal thing, with green furry leaves. Such an old
country traveling tradition. Always carry a plant. Always stay rooted
to somewhere. And I looked around that gate of late and weary ones
and thought, this is the world I want to live in. The shared world. Not
a single person in this gate – once the crying of confusion stopped –
seemed apprehensive about any other person. They took the cookies.
I wanted to hug all those other women too. This can still happen
anywhere. Not everything is lost.

Chapter 5
Trust and Inner Healing
By Pat R. Farrell, OSF

For the last 10 years I have been walking with people who have endured severe trauma. It is a path that chose me, beginning with my experience in a war zone in El Salvador. I was surrounded by the tragic effects of violence, seen in people I had come to know and love and in a country that had come to feel like my own. My experience was not one of distinguishing inner trauma and outer trauma, or personal and collective wounding. There was simply a flow of life and experience, an impact of suffering, the effects of which were interpenetrating and indistinguishable on the levels of personal and social pain. While most of my healing work has been in the area of individual trauma therapy, I have an inner eye always turned towards the larger social ripples of what each individual has experienced. I hear in every person's longing to be at peace with a painful experience the cry of a larger world to assimilate and make peace with its shadowed history.

An individual's journey of inner healing from trauma is a dance of approach and avoidance. The urge for expression and the need for someone to know the secret, unspeakable pain of a traumatic event continually pushes its way to the surface of consciousness. At the same time another inner force strains to keep feelings and memories at bay. There is a need to deny and to distance, to silence, to bury, to disconnect, to avoid. It is an exhausting dialectic. Underneath it all, however, I believe there is a relentless drive towards healing and wholeness that is the hallmark of human existence. Something at the core of us is programmed towards wholeness and wellbeing and drives us in myriad ways, including hurtful and self-sabotaging ways, towards healing and peace.

The journey is one of incredible courage, with a decision at some level to move beyond the experience of being a victim. It usually comes out of a readiness that is long in the ripening. Sometimes that readiness is not even conscious, as a person moves seemingly against her will, emotionally kicking and screaming in a therapeutic direction. But I do believe that the unfolding process responds to an inner timing described so well by the Chinese proverb that says "When the student is ready the master appears." The readiness can show itself in the form of buried memories that suddenly surface, in a melt down sort of emotional crisis experience, in a growing desire to seek healing, in converging circumstances that nudge one to move past accustomed resistance, or in any variety of ways. The continuous movement towards healing might be the hidden, apparently dormant activity of the inner spirit simply gathering the energy necessary for the unfolding to begin. Or it might be conscious and decisive and active. But it is a holistic dynamic in which body, mind and spirit somehow strain towards harmony and integration. The fractured self begins to re-member, haltingly.

The early concerns of healing tend to focus on safety and control. The perceived threat can be internal. The need for control might manifest in a preoccupation with the containment of unmanageable emotional states, of intrusive images and disquieting memories, of nightmares, of undesired acting out of aspects of the trauma. On the other hand, the threat is often a real, external danger from which the person seeks protection. Refugees flee to safety. Battered wives, often ambivalently, might leave an abusive relationship. Abused children are frequently taken from the home. A minimal sense of safety and control is usually the initial step which makes it possible for the person to let down her guard sufficiently to be able to squarely confront a painful experience.

 A further step in the healing process is that of reconstructing the experience, of remembering and acknowledging the reality of what actually happened. It is a raw and arduous process, facilitated usually through a healing relationship. For the unspeakable to be spoken and to fall on human, caring ears is deeply healing, albeit deeply painful as well. There is a particular emotional impact that occurs when a person's hidden, private pain is compassionately held by another human being. Suddenly it becomes more real as it is reflected by the other. It can be released and mourned. It can be felt, acknowledged, witnessed and received. The process gradually brings perspective and insight to what is often experienced as a muddy confusion of memory and emotion, of fact and of perception. There may never be total clarity, but the fog begins to lift. The narrative of victim is therapeutically rewritten in a process of empowerment.

The releasing and mourning of a painful past continues the dance of approach and avoidance. It is very difficult. One of the most significant resources in that process is the body. Given the fact that so much of the fight and flight response of the autonomic nervous system that gets spontaneously triggered in trauma is held in the body, release is also largely physiological. Healing and release is a multi-dimensional, holistic experience but I am convinced that its primary escape valve is the body, also the point of access to other dimensions. The retinue of body work modalities recently available

as therapeutic tools is a veritable gold mine. It would seem that the evolutionary process is speeding up human healing with the discovery of newer body-based practices as well as the re-discovery of ancient ones. I can no longer imagine doing trauma work without them.
In all of the above mentioned, the traumatized person is gradually reconnecting. After the isolation of secrecy and denial, the person begins to venture into a more trusting way of relating to self and to another. She reconnects gradually with her body and with her feelings. And little by little there is also a movement to reconnect with a larger community. She begins to emerge with a re-written script of expectations of herself and of life. The myth of invulnerability is gone forever. A view of the world as a safe, predictable, firmly ordered reality has been replaced by an acceptance of insecurity and ambiguity. Paradoxically, there often emerges an expanding of consciousness as well. The painful cracking open of the limits of body, mind, and spirit is truly a crisis: danger and opportunity. The danger is, of course, that the healing process can be resisted and never actively undertaken. The opportunity is that trauma can push someone beyond the normal physical, mental, emotional, and spiritual protective confines of existence into a more expansive way of being in the world.

As I describe all of this, I am aware again of those larger, social ripples of healing that accompany an individual's healing process. There are sometimes dramatic, sometimes imperceptible shifts within the family or larger social context of the person who engages in a healing process, even if that process is unknown to the others connected to the traumatic event. Healing and forgiveness creates a release in victim and perpetrator alike. I could explore that at length. However, what I'd like to focus on are the parallel healing processes of personal and social transformation.

Any thinking person in the United States right now would acknowledge that we are in crisis. Yet we mostly go about our day to day endeavors as if that were not the case. Judith Herman says it well in her book Trauma and Recovery: "The knowledge of horrible events periodically intrudes into public awareness but is rarely retained for long. Denial, repression, and dissociation operate on a social as well as an individual level. The study of psychological trauma has an 'underground' history. Like traumatized people, we have been cut off from the knowledge of our past. Like traumatized people we need to understand the past in order to reclaim the present and the future. … In the absence of strong political movements for human rights, the active process of bearing witness inevitably gives way to the active process of forgetting."

The horrible events are legion: Abu Ghrab, 9/11, the 650,000+ civilians killed in Iraq in the war, the voluntary relinquishment of civil liberties by the American people in the name of security, the disproportionate guilt of the U.S. in the carbon emissions creating global warming, the treatment of prisoners at Guantanamo, the euphemistic expressions used to deny the CIA's continued use of torture, our own weapons of mass destruction and the billions of dollars spent on warfare as U.S. health and education languish. Truly it is a crisis: again, danger and opportunity. The danger is in our inability and unwillingness to look at a reality we would rather deny. Like traumatized individuals, our society finds its own collective vulnerability and capacity for evil too painful to embrace. We go to great lengths to establish the sense of safety and control that will enable us to let down our guard and to see the truth of our experience. Yet ultimately, the collective transformative task is to lay aside the myth of invulnerability and to embrace the simple reality of the limits, insecurity and ambiguities that we share with the rest of the human family.

The exaggerated efforts to create security from terrorists and other such bogeymen are reflected not only in programs of homeland security and national defense. We see them in the way we tend to treat the more vulnerable and disenfranchised in our midst. Those on welfare who have been the victims of economic disparity are discredited and/or rendered invisible. Minorities are shunned and feared. In general, those who so obviously embody pain force us all to look at what we instinctively deny, so we want them out of sight. The U.S. has the highest rate of incarceration of any developed country in the world. And for those whose conduct is the most abhorrent to us we seek the death penalty so that they are permanently out of sight and so that we do not have to look into the face of our own potential for evil.

In contrast, I recently heard someone give an account of having witnessed the ritual a certain group of Native Americans undergoes when someone in the community has murdered someone else. The community gathers and in their presence a tribal elder paints the perpetrator's face and body with the charcoal of an extinguished fire. That person is then mandated to move within the daily activities of the community without bathing or washing off the charcoal, continually praying to the spirit of the victim for healing and forgiveness. The community, on the other hand, is to shun the person, neither acknowledging his presence nor speaking to him, though he is always visible among them. At the end of a certain designated time period the community gathers again with the perpetrator and celebrates a ritual called "the circle of tears". There is drumming, dancing, praying and ceremonial wailing. The charcoal is washed from his face with the tears of those who weep and he is re-admitted to the community where normal communication and interactions are resumed.

The Native American ritual does not go the way of "out of sight, out of mind". Denial and demonization are discouraged. But the disconnect is acted out. The fractured relationships are acknowledged. The final ritual is a collective mourning exercise needed by both the murderer and the community. The ritualized reconnection is quite significantly a community event, holistically engaging body, mind and spirit. It seems there are deeply transformative lessons for us to learn here.

Just as in the healing of individual trauma, there is an incredible emotional impact in having unspeakable events both spoken and heard. A community's history needs to be told and the process is arduous. Public acknowledgement of pain and guilt is essential in the healing of collective suffering. I personally experienced the tremendously significant effect of the publication of the findings of the Truth Commission after El Salvador's civil war. The truth of massacres and atrocities needed to be told. The world needed to hear. I also experienced the widespread indignation and outrage at the refusal of members of the government and military to acknowledge the truth of the commission's findings and their subsequent declaration of amnesty so as to avoid consequences. It was an obstacle to real peace. The process used in South Africa after the civil war lent itself much more to genuine healing, reconciliation and peace. Amnesty was offered only to those who publicly confessed to the abuses they had committed. The real danger to peace and reconciliation is continued denial.

For most of us the national and world crises feel more like "danger" than like "opportunity". And yet, I do believe that just as the human spirit is programmed towards wholeness and relentlessly pursues it, even through errant ways, so also is our collective spirit. I trust that a readiness is ripening in the human family to move beyond denial and to confront the reality of our own vulnerability and capacity for evil. We desperately need to re-connect. We need to embrace the vulnerable in our world. We need to muster the courage to relate to evil and collective acting out with non-violent listening and understanding of differences. And we need to draw strength from the resource of nature, the body of our planet and of our God. I trust that there is at the very least an apparently dormant gathering of our collective human strength for the unfolding of the future that is drawing us. Hopefully more and more of us can move in globally transformative directions consciously, actively, decisively, so that the limits of our collective consciousness might be cracked open to new capacities for peace and healing.

Chapter 6
Post Traumatic Stress & Inner Healing
By Brenda

My name is Brenda and I have a story I would like to share. It's a story about a part of my life that I spent years trying to justify, avoid, forget, run away from, ignore, laugh off, hide away...whatever. What follows is the recounting of my struggles with Post-Traumatic Stress Disorder (PTSD) which I acquired during military service during the 1991 Persian Gulf War, and my time of service in the United States Army.

Let me just begin this sharing by saying that this is not an attempt to gain sympathy or to malign the government or military for how life turned out after my time in service. No, the point of this sharing is to let people know that healing from a traumatic experience is possible! I won't tell you the process is pain-free or easy, but I can tell you it is worth the HARD effort to become more healthy and whole. During the course of my trauma work I encountered many of my fears and tears that I had kept locked away. I also experienced many frustrations and episodes of anger, helplessness, hopelessness and sometimes rage. There were even days when I thought it would be a lot easier to pull the earth over me and call it a day because the shame, guilt, and sadness felt too overpowering. It has taken me several years to recognize, accept, and now only fairly recently deal with the PTSD symptoms that are a part of my life. Through intensive counseling, prayer, compassionate, loving friends and listening to my own inner wisdom, I've learned that the PTSD I have isn't my "enemy", something to be evaded, on guard against, or distrustful of, as I once did. I've come to understand that it is a reality for me and it needs to be embraced as a presence in my life because it's a part of ME and worthy of attention, understanding, tenderness, forgiveness and compassion.

I've heard it said, "The longest journey anyone will ever take is the journey inward." I don't remember who said it, but I've found it to be very true in my life. For years I found it to be the loneliest and most painful journey as well. What counselors, my religious sisters and friends have helped me to see over time is that the journey didn't have to be so lonely. I had options, though at the time I couldn't see them or wouldn't see them for whatever reasons. It's true, I guess I could have invited people to "walk" with me, to hold me up when I felt like crumbling under the weight of despair and hopelessness: The truth is though, that my "secrets" and the anxieties that went along with those "secrets" blinded me to the point that I couldn't see, let alone choose the option of accompaniment. It felt too risky! It terrified me to think about how people I loved and respected would act toward me if they knew about some of the things I was a part of and did in the war. I told myself they wouldn't understand; they couldn't! Besides I didn't need their pity or their judgments. No, I determined it was better to go this alone. I'm sad to say this kind of thinking imprisoned me, entombed me, for almost fifteen years.

During the course of my life a lack of understanding and acceptance of the trauma I'd encountered during the war began to take a heavy toll on every aspect of my daily life. My relationships, my faith life, my work, my studies, and eventually my eating habits, relaxation and sleep time began to suffer. When I saw this happening I panicked! Frequently, I would say to myself everything I learned when learning how to be a "good soldier." Things like, "Don't ever let them see you cry!!" (That was cardinal rule number one) "Deal with it!!" "Maintain your control!!" **DISCIPLINE, DISCIPLINE, DISCIPLINE!!!**

This kind of thinking had served me very well in past so I couldn't understand why wasn't it working now. Life felt so heavy for me! I didn't seem to be able to deal with the small or the larger things in life anymore. I felt so out of control of everything, but most especially my emotions. I began to notice that I didn't trust my feelings, thoughts or judgments and I began to notice that I really didn't trust anyone else either. This awareness only intensified my sense of low self-esteem and loneliness. I was caught in a vicious cycle that quickly sent me spiraling downward into what felt like an abyss. I couldn't "get a grip" on anything! It was like nothing felt real or solid or safe anymore. I was losing ground fast. I knew it, but felt helpless to do anything about it! It was at this point my religious sisters invited me to take some time to look at what was happening inside of me.

The truth is, I didn't see the "invitation" for what it was at that time—a gift! Instead I felt betrayed, suspicious, angry, defensive, embarrassed, and humiliated. At the time of my "meltdown" I wasn't a professed member of my religious congregation (I was in the military before I entered religious life) and figured this was their way of telling me I wasn't ever going to be a permanent member. A barrage of angry thoughts assaulted me during this time. At my lowest point I had packed my belongings and set them on the bed because I was leaving! What do they know about how I'm feeling anyway, is what I told myself. In the solitude of my room I sat staring at those bags. I was trying to work up the courage to walk away, to leave, to say good bye to the only thing that had managed to remain important and alive in me. Where everything else had lost life and love, only this remained alive and worth loving. Could I walk away from it? Did I REALLY want to? My community's love for me, their concern and their faith in me seemed to be the only thing that kept me grounded when everything else seemingly was drifting away. The time had come – do I walk away again or do I stay and face myself? By the grace of God, I gave leadership my feeble, but committed "yes" to facing myself. I would ask and stand ready to receive help.

I spent the next seven months in intense counseling, trying to come to terms with the "ghosts" that haunted my sleep and the "monster" that seemingly wouldn't go away. It was a painful time for me! The counseling required me to talk about so much of what I tried for fifteen years to forget. I often times remarked to my counselor that "talking about memories or situations won't change things." I saw no point in dredging up the past and picking it a part. How absolutely wrong I was!

> *If you are able to experience the pain without giving it the power to take you down emotionally, then you will soon find yourself making big strides in the healing of past wounds.*

As I told you in the opening paragraph, I was a soldier in the Army during Operation Desert Storm. My military occupational specialty (MOS) was 91 Charlie or Licensed Practical Nurse. I had just gotten my Charlie identifier (nursing) in mid December of 1990. I was activated for the Persian Gulf the same day that I graduated from the school. My first nursing experience post-graduation was going to be battlefield nursing, and I was terrified!

Despite the fact that I was trained as a nurse I was first and foremost a "soldier" and I should never forget that. I was told that I may be assigned to do different duties that had nothing to do with my MOS, but that I had an obligation and a duty to obey any and all orders. People's lives depended on me and how well I obeyed orders. I understood this (I thought) and vowed to do my part no matter what. People's lives— WOW, this is no small thing! I remember telling myself that I was going to work hard and save as many lives as I could by being a competent, caring, 91 Charlie. I thought often about the pledge I said the day of my graduation from nursing school "provide care, protect life and to make every effort to do no harm." My pledge was my word.

We arrived in Saudi Arabia January 2nd of 1991. The war had not started yet. My unit was in a holding pattern somewhere in the desert. The days were unmercifully long and the nights were even longer as we waited for whatever to happen. I was restless, homesick, scared, and bored because all there was to do was sit and think about home or what could happen. They asked for volunteers to be on a convoy so I volunteered. It would give me something to do and I could travel about meeting people and seeing different places. Besides, loading and unloading the 5 ton trucks with medical equipment would provide me with some needed exercise. There were 25 of us on the convoy team. Since I was attached to the unit (it was where I was assigned) and didn't know anyone I figured it'd be a way to make friends. We worked hard as a team and we became fairly close as we'd share stories about our lives and our families back home. We even got to the point where we'd share our anxieties about what it might be like to be in a war. (Soldiers never share fears.)

One evening around supper, about two weeks into our convoy life, we were eating our meals-ready-to-eat (MREs) when the sirens sounded alerting us to an attack. (The war had only recently begun by this time.) Because I was the lowest ranking person in the group (most expendable) my position was in the forward. We took up our fighting positions behind some of the crates we were loading, locked and loaded our M-16's and we were given the order to fire on anything that moved. My heart was pounding, my hands were shaking, I could barely breathe! This was the first gunfire attack I had been in – bomb attacks were more common. I heard bullets ricocheting off the buildings and the steel of the equipment that surrounded us. I heard the deafening blasts of the M-80 machine guns in the towers a few yards from our position. It's strange because as fast as everything was happening I felt like everything I saw and did was in slow motion; people's movements, their facial expressions, hand signals, they were all in slow motion, just like in the movies! I remember thinking how heavy my body felt, like I was encased in lead or something. The bullets were whizzing past me, it was crazy! At my 11 o'clock position I saw three forms running toward us. I remember steadying my weapon on the crate I was hiding behind, visualizing a torso, taking a deep breath and holding it. My finger was on the trigger and slowly I squeezed until three or four rounds were spent. Through my weapon site I saw a form fall to the ground, make some jerking movements, then no movement at all.

To this day I still don't recall much of anything that immediately took place after that firefight. No one on the convoy team ever talked about it. The war did go on and so did we. What else was there to do?

> *On dealing with insomnia:*
>
> *Find an affirmation that you can repeat until the mind stops its tantrum*

Despite the fact that history says Desert Storm was a "short war" with minimal casualties, I'm afraid I would beg to differ with that final analysis. If the truth were known I'm sure every troop that was there has a story to tell about a traumatizing event(s) that reshaped their lives to one degree or another. Quite probably some wounds are not understood or are kept hidden like mine were.

The first step in my healing process wasn't necessarily admitting that I had some issues that I needed help with. It was more that I was open to the possibility that maybe I could be happy again for longer than a few fleeting minutes. I wanted to be happy! I was so very tired of life feeling so heavy. I wanted to feel good about myself because some-where deep inside of me, I knew I was good. Just that sliver of open-ness was enough to change my life for the better. I found POWER in nothing to lose.

What I found MOST helpful during the process of my healing were counselors and friends who abstained from judgment of me. God knows I had done enough of that for myself! Those who "walked" with me didn't judge anything I said instead they offered a listening ear. They didn't give me advice; they showed me compassion. And instead of trying to "fix me" they allowed me to fall apart, but stood near enough to help me up when I felt ready to stand on my own. My coun-selors, religious sisters, and friends were paramount in the process of healing.

I don't think I have completed this journey of healing by any means. I think it's a life-long, ongoing process. I'm sure of this though, wher-ever we are and wherever we want to go in life will require risk and companions to help us along the way. We are human beings and some-times our greatest strength is the knowledge that we are all fragile to some extent. We are created in relationship (Father, Son and Holy Spirit) and we are meant to be relational in matters of LIVING. We are also stronger than we think, wiser than we dare to believe, and more connected to each other than we care to admit.

If there is a blessing in having Post-Traumatic Stress Disorder, I would have to say that it's the realization that I need caring people in my life to keep me grounded and to keep me striving toward the person I was/am created to be.

The work of healing is HARD, but like the birthing of a baby, the la-bor of the birth soon becomes just a faint memory and you spend the rest of your life enjoying the beauty and life you helped bring into the world. The TRUTH I've come to know is that there is life after trauma and its sweet and rich and worth the struggle to be FREE!

On dealing with Post Traumatic Stress Triggers:

*Why does something as simple as music
become a source of trauma?*

*The simple answer is that you got triggered. Music touches
your soul - and some music just takes us into spaces that are
traumatic. There was something about the music that evoked
a feeling and when you were not 'heard' or felt discounted it
spiraled you into deeper wells.*

*I feel you are reliving an old feeling which is why it is so out of
proportion to the actual events going on.
Talk with the folks that you feel so discounted by. It will help you
live in the present. They don't have to take care of you; you need
them to hear you. And before returning to the group, you need to
talk to yourself and make sure that self stays in reality.*

*The past is overwhelming the present
and therefore is out of proportion.*

*I see this as another level of healing. It is time for the adult you to
protect the 'child' within you, not by letting her get triggered, but
by letting her know you are in relationship with her. In this world
you are safe and so is she.*

*Since we really can't change thought patterns once they get
triggered, use your breath and your sense of smell to keep you
in the present. And when the destructive thoughts start coming,
don't try to get rid of them, rather let your breathing keep you
current.*

*From a spiritual perspective, the counsel is always not to look at
the destructive thinking, but to claim the Power within you even
as you have those thoughts. God is always present even when we
may not think that is possible.*

*Do something good for you this weekend that will restore your
body, mind, soul and emotions. Take it easy today. Let your body
be in water if you can. (bath tub will do). Just feel yourself held in
the water of life and know there are so many others who hold you
also.*

Words of Wisdom from a Spiritual Amma – Jean Springer

Chapter 7
Healing from Domestic Violence
Patricia S. Castillo, LMSW

Trauma, transformation and healing...is happening!

Family violence, spousal abuse, intimate partner violence, dating violence and relationship violence are all terms used interchangeably when describing beatings and abuse by one partner in a relationship done to the other for purposes of gaining and maintaining power and control over them. Sometimes this is achieved by the mere use of strategically placed and selected words as well.

Family violence affects people of every race and economic class. Yet, many who suffer from its effects are ashamed to tell anyone. Society has trained people to hide the violence. Perpetrators have learned to isolate the people they abuse. A lot of attitudes need to be changed if we are to be effective in ending domestic violence. ***One person can make a difference***.

All of us can and need to reach out to the person who is being battered in an intimate relationship. A few words of caring and concern, genuinely expressed, can and does work miracles.

I remember countless times saying to survivors, "When was the last time you had a good night's sleep?" This question usually provokes a meltdown due to their exhaustion, sleep deprivation and fear. Their immediate response amidst the tears and sobbing is "How did you know?" I know because perpetrators of abuse want us to be tired, drained, overwhelmed, and to lose our spirit. We're easy targets under those kinds of conditions. Many have been sleep deprived since they were children because they have lived in homes where the violence was akin to a war zone. Maybe they have never had a good night's sleep. They've lived in home-grown violence that started in their childhood: perhaps even in the womb.

What is most heartbreaking is to see how this part of the manipulation and domination process impedes their ability to make good, informed decisions about their lives, their children's lives, and their situation of victimization. That is what society demands of them. Society expects them to "Hurry up, leave the abuser". We mistakenly say to survivors what we think are "encouraging statements" like "Shoot, if I was you, I would have left a long time ago,—I wouldn't be putting up with that kind of behavior if I were you".

Well, we're not them and honestly, we truly don't know what we would do until we're staring the abuse and the abuser in the face, cross-eyed from the violence, threats, lack of resources, family pressures, sleep deprivation and depression. On top of that, there are two or three kids hanging from our skirts demanding our love and attention. Ironically, this is the time when survivors are mostly isolated and at the same time when they most need us, their support system.

Another irony is that as part of the social order, we also expect members of our society to be coupled, to be part of a family, to procreate, to support their spouse and to do all we can to keep our families together. Apart from fear, this is mostly why survivors of family violence go back to their abusers an average of 5-7 times.

Leaving an abuser is a process that is dangerous, calls for courage, requires support, takes time, and must include information about resources. Most survivors who are murdered are usually killed when in the process of "getting out" or "leaving the abuser."

So yes, this is when a circle of family and friends is most needed. This is when the laws we've enacted must be enforced. This is when a powerful message must resound: "Your use of violence is wrong and criminal." The violent perpetrator needs to hear and see this message projected at them from all aspects of society. The perpetrators of family violence must know that we, the community, expect a change from them and that their chosen victim will not face their ravaging violence alone without the support of their community.

Organizing in my community for this to happen for all survivors of family violence, has blessed me with the privilege of witnessing the freeing of hundreds of survivors who have gotten out of abusive, violent relationships. It is happening every day.

That is why doing this for 27 years has been worth it. Knowing that there are survivors around me everywhere, from all walks of life, all races, all colors, all religions, all levels of intelligence, and all types of lifestyles who now live violence free, merits everything we are willing to risk investing !!!

Most men in our world are worn out and sadly, mostly silenced about the violence perpetrated by a few of them. It doesn't behoove men to stay silent about their opposition to violence perpetrated by their friends, family members, or co-workers. They need to join with women and speak out against family violence.

This is beginning to happen for—and with—men. Their hearts and souls have been wounded by the violence wreaking havoc on our families. It's not enough for them to be well-meaning men who don't abuse those whom they love. What we need from men is their voices raised, taking the risk of speaking out against violence. It is a blessing to be able to testify that I have seen them do so over the past few years. While I know that much of the work they do on their issues happens in their circles, I also know that they are willing to give us their hand in peace to struggle alongside us to stop family violence.

In another emerging area of need, men, who fall prey to relationship violence from their spouses or intimate partners must be believed and supported in their efforts to get safe, be protected and live free from their perpetrators' violence. Most importantly, we must not judge or ridicule them when they are victimized. The damage done to men in their relationships is devastating as well.

Below are some possible conversation starters for talking about domestic violence with family, friends, or coworkers—anybody, really:

"*Manita*, (sister), is everything O.K. at home?"

"*Vecina* (Neighbor), I heard some shouting and crying coming from your house last night, is something going on I can help you with?"

"*Amiga*, (friend) you don't deserve to be treated that way, no matter what happened between the two of you!"

"*Prima,* (cousin), I'm sorry that your family isn't helping you right now, but can I help by giving you a lift to a friend's house, the shelter, or the police department where you can talk to someone about available resources?"

"*Hermano*,(brother)no tengas verguenza pedir ayuda,, don't be embarrassed to seek help. Your right to have safety and protection for yourself and your kids is just as valid and no one has the right to treat you this way."

"*Comadre, no aguantes el maltrato de tu pareja. Hay gente que quieren ayudar!*" (Friend, abuse and violence from those you love is not acceptable. There are people who want to help!)

"Grandma, I want you to spend your later years in peace and comfort, not having to be afraid of your every movement or word."

"Co-worker, we'll give you a couple of days off so you can go and get the protective order, press charges and make arrangements to live somewhere safe. Don't worry; your job will be here when you return."

"Momma, I know you love him, but his violence will continue as long as he avoids taking responsibility and blames others for his aggressive actions. You don't provoke the violence; he chooses to hit you in order to control you and have power over you."

Ya Basta con la violencia! (The violence has to stop!) *ya estuvo padre*, (There have been more than enough excuses for not acting). The most common excuse is, "It's none of my business." It is my business; it is your business, and it is everybody's business when that kind of violence is happening to someone we know, someone we love, or someone who is within our reach. We can start with a simple question, "Is someone at home hurting you"?

A hug may cause unexpected tears to be shed; a touch of the hand may result in a surprising revelation of violence lurking beneath facades of "normalcy".

The "it's not my problem" attitude and way of thinking can get people killed. We continue to see an overwhelming number of images in the media of men, women, and children ending up as consequential tragedies of the evils of domestic violence. Sadder still is that it doesn't have to be that way. We are not born violent. *¡La violencia no es nuestro destino!* (Violence is not our destiny.) We don't have to stay "for the children". *El niño aprende lo que vive.* (Our children learn what they live.) We can and do raise non-violent children. We have to do it everywhere, all the time. *Así como la violencia afecta a todos, la paz también nos puede afectar y cambiar.* (Just as violence affects us all, so too can peace change us.) It's worth the risk of opening our hearts to the work of ending domestic violence. We need to be moved by those who have died and in their memory work for peace. *Comprométete a buscar y vivir en Paz.* (Commit to working for and living in Peace.)

In all of my years of working as an advocate for women who have been battered and abused by someone who professes to love them, they've consistently asked to just be able to live in peace, have their kids grow up in a peaceful home and neighborhood and to be able to experience peace in the intimate relationships with those they love.

An old Chinese prayer from the Tao Te Ching reminds us:

There's no peace in the world
without peace in the nations;
there's no peace in the nations,
without peace in the town,
there's no peace in the town
without peace in the home
and there's no peace in the home
without peace
in the heart.

Do we have the heart to struggle for this kind of peace? You bet we do; I've witnessed people in my city do it for the past 27 years. Our struggle has just started. Unfortunately, it isn't until people have died that we realize just how valuable, precious, and priceless we all are. Let's live what we've learned from these deaths. Our contact information is in the resource section of this book. We hope to hear from you. Please, get involved in the work to end violence in families. We need your energy, creativity, *ganas* (desire), commitment, diversity, youthfulness, wisdom, and enthusiasm to transform this violence into what we most hunger for – LOVE.

Chapter 8
Grief Work and Inner Healing
By Liz Cummins

The journey of inner healing often begins with the journey of grief.

In the beginning you weep.
The starting point for many things is grief, at the place where endings
seem so absolute. One would think it should be otherwise, but the
pain of closing is antecedent to every new opening in our life.[1]
Belden Lane, The Solace of Fierce Landscapes

Grief is the natural response to the experience of loss and pain; it
throws us into a place that is foreign and often terrifying – familiar and
safe boundaries are blurred or gone. It is a fierce landscape. It brings
us to limits, to starkness, to our own vulnerability. It brings us into
liminal space – the space between – the place
we instinctively try to leave: to run from or to
explain. From that place, grief offers us another
way of knowing life.

I came to the desert Southwest over 20 years
ago now, knowing only that it was time to leave
the familiar heartland of the Midwest for a
'fierce landscape'. What I did not know was that I
needed to come to the desert to grieve and
to heal. Slowly the desert began showing me
the narrow and constricted life I had chosen
in holding tightly to a lifetime of betrayal and
loss. The spaciousness of the desert and its
authenticity attracted and beckoned me, inviting
me to explore another way of living.

The healing that the desert has been offering these
many years is learning to live intentionally within
the Mystery and rhythm of life
– to disarm and soften my
heart, to live gratefully and
graciously as a part of the
great web of life.

Over the years I've come to some beliefs about the mystery of grieving and healing:

- ❖ that loss and grief and healing are part of the fabric of life in which we all share
- ❖ that in isolating our personal pain and loss from that of all life, we separate ourselves from the healing it offers
- ❖ that loss and grief bring us to the threshold of a new spaciousness and new dimension of human life
- ❖ that healing is an ever deepening capacity for compassion and mercy

In this Chapter, I share some reflections from my experience of this journey and the challenge it offers to participate fully in the adventure of life.

Healing begins with our specific experiences of loss and grief – *In the beginning you weep* - but it is much more. Loss and pain and grief are places of entry into our own vulnerability – the liminal space we need to enter and the space we fear. Loss can be varied: illness, dying, death, betrayal, divorce, abuse, aging, disappointment, limitations. Our initial response to any loss is to protect ourselves from the overwhelming pain: to add layers of armor around our heart, to shut down and withdraw and distance ourselves. Grief calls us to enter into the pain of loss – the fierce landscape – something that sounds absurd and impossible.

> *. . . the logical, rational response is not always reliable; wisdom is often held by the absurd.*

When I am with people who are grieving and where entering into the pain sounds very absurd and impossible, I found a simple analogy helpful. I ask them to remember the advice given if the car they are driving begins to slide on ice; they all know it: turn in the direction of the skid. Then I tell them my experience: my car is sliding, I am repeating in my mind 'turn in the direction of the skid' and I automatically turn the opposite way and end up in the ditch. Now, I am grateful for this experience: the car was not damaged; I was not hurt since the ditch was filled with soft new snow; I was rescued by AAA in a timely manner – and I began to learn a valuable truth about life: the logical, rational response is not always reliable; wisdom is often held by the absurd. Healing seldom comes in the form we recognize and welcome.

Hiking the desert has taught me a way to enter a fierce landscape. It is essential to enter the desert with respect and attention: respect for the hostile environment and its rhythm of life; and attention to where

I am hiking and to my surroundings. The desert is not romantic; it is indifferent and cares little about us. Alertness, stepping lightly and without stumbling is a desert skill. Over the years the desert has been teaching me to relate to it from within it, honoring the current of life that organizes it, coming into a harmony with it instead of struggling against it. This is always the challenge: to meet the hostile environment with a kind of non-resistance, to enter a more open relationship with it, to enter the desert with 'eyes wide open'.

Entering the fierce landscape of grief with 'eyes wide open' is entering intentionally, with a willingness to meet the pain of loss with mercy. Each time we touch our grief with compassion and mercy instead of hatred and fear, we let healing in. This is the mystery and the alchemy of healing: the pain of loss and grief will open our hearts, season us and create us capable of compassion for others.

The Persian poet-mystic Hafiz speaks of this mystery[2]:

> Don't surrender your loneliness
> So quickly.
> Let it cut more deep.
> Let it ferment and season you
> As few human
> Or even divine ingredients can.
> Something missing in my heart tonight
> Has made my eyes so soft,
> My voice
> So tender,
> My need of God
> Absolutely
> Clear.

The fierce landscape of grief offers a contemplative way of knowing and living life: knowing life from within it, recognizing and participating in its rhythm instead of being outside and over against it. Meeting our grief with mercy slows us down and draws us within. In that inner silence and stillness we experience our hearts softening and expanding; there is a new spaciousness where we discover a compassion for all life and a glimpse of its oneness.

In this new spaciousness we also discover deep within us a vast underground pool, holding all the losses we have not acknowledged. Stephen Levine calls this reservoir of losses our 'unattended sorrow.'[3] It is this unfinished business of loss and grief that dampens and drains our life energy and our hope. It is often so familiar to us that we do not notice it or attend to it.

I have found that a daily practice of sending mercy into the sorrows of the day helps me attend to the residue of loss. This is my personal form of reflection on my day, and it is in two parts: in the early evening I spend a few minutes in my little garden, just being with it, noticing what is growing, walking among the herbs and letting the garden and the earth quiet me. Then before I go to bed, I sit in stillness and let the events and feelings of the day surface, meeting each with mercy and letting it go. This daily practice is a source of healing for me. I encourage those I meet to create their own personal practice that will attend to their daily losses.

I am noticing something else that flows from this daily practice: I am becoming less afraid of loss and grief. In some way I am learning how to befriend my grief; the instinctive move to turn away from it, to protect and insulate myself from it is not so automatic now. Becoming able to look at it with loving kindness instead of fear and dread reveals that my personal pain of loss is not mine alone; is a shared grief, a part of the loss and grief of all life. In the way of Mystery, loss and grief, which so often isolate us from others become the way of bringing us together in a deeper experience of the unity of life.

Today our planet and all life stand at the place of endings; the grief of our world is enormous and deep and overwhelming. When each of us personally meets our pain and loss and grief with compassion and mercy instead of fear and hatred, we touch with mercy the pain of the world - we let healing enter our shared lives.

[1] Lane, Belden C. The Solace of Fierce Landscapes. NY: Oxford University Press, 1988. p. 5.
[2] 'Eyes So Soft' by Hafiz; as quoted in "Grieving as Sacred Space" by Richard Rohr, OFM. Sojourners Magazine, January-February 2002 (Vol. 31, No. 1) p. 24.
[3] Levine, Stephen. Unattended Sorrow: Recovering from Loss and Reviving the Heart. NY: Rodale Books, 2005. p.5

Chapter 9
Healing From the Inside Out
Catherine L. Cuasay

In the heart of a seed, buried deep, so deep...
A dear little plant lay fast asleep.
"Wake" said the voice of the raindrops light.
"Wake" said the voice of the sunshine bright
And the little plant came out to see
What a wide and wonderful world might be.

Like dear little plants we all emerge fresh, hopeful, and vulnerable. We need the incubation of a nurturing space surrounding us with a fertile bed of soil softened by gentle rain and warmed by a blanket of steady sunlight beams. But even given rare and fine external conditions for growth, we also must have cultivated enough safety within the core of our seed world to become attuned to the signals when the time is ripe to venture forth. Growth involves the necessary separation from that which is being outgrown.

This seed poem is one of the first I ever learned in English and I do not think I have outgrown it yet. What seemed to make it infinitely more interesting and deeply ingrained in my memory were the gestures which accompanied the rhyme. These simple movements made it a full body experience set apart from a Mother Goose world where the only other contenders for words combined with gestures at the time were the Itsy-Bitsy Spider, This Little Piggy Went to Market, and the Hokey Pokey. Teachers well know that the more sensory venues with which a lesson is offered, the longer and more completely it can be retained because there are more pathways to knowing and mastering it. Mental health therapists have also learned that there can be many tags leading back to the same memory of an event whether it is a treasured or traumatic one. These tags or "triggers" could be colors, images, arrangements of objects, sounds, smells, tastes, physical sensations, or textures. Each sensory path expands or enriches the dimensions of an internalized experience. It is along these very paths that the arts appeal to us and can be vital to helping us understand emotional experiences.

Paintings, poetry, letters, lullabies, songs, symphonies, gestures, movement, dance, sculpture, and collage are all ways of communicating about human experience and as such are all paths to accessing emotions. The value of these alternative paths to knowing and understanding is most evident in situations where words alone are inadequate to aptly relate an experience. If breathtaking physical scenes such as sunsets, beachscapes, and lightning storms frequently elicit comments that there are no words to fully describe them: how, then, can we grasp unseen experiences such as love, fear, and sorrow?

Natalie Rogers, a giant in the field of Person Centered Expressive Therapy, often begins her workshops with a shift away from the usual wordy introductions in mouthfuls of name, rank and demographic information. She instead opts for a visit with each participant around the circle and invites them to offer their name accompanied by a gesture or a sound that conveys how they are feeling in the moment. This is certainly a different way of coming to know others by encountering information about how they feel rather than where they live or what they do. The challenge is to cast aside the customary societal masks and allow others to meet a more authentic self. Natalie regards the arts as vessels through which our expressions can be poured. She teaches a powerful concept of The Creative Connection, which is a spiraling deepening path to understanding experience.

Take for instance the concept of growth and the seed poem I first learned. Beginning with the words in mind ...in the heart of a seed... little plant...fast asleep: what images enter my mind? I might draw an almond shaped seed with brown earth around, enough for roots to come out and sink in and a layer above showing where the sunlight skims the surface of the soil and where the raindrops land. Studying the drawn image of "the heart of a seed" and choosing one part to explore in body movement, what shape might my body take to be in slumber somewhere deep and protected? Perhaps I feel that in a fetal pose, I curl up like a nested egg or a burrowed bunny, but as I assume that position, pouring those words and images into movement, I am also aware of other sensations: warmth, safety, containment, being centered/grounded. Emotionally I feel expectant—resting, but waiting to be awakened.

To further enrich my experience of this seed-heart place, I could also consider the dimension of sound. What would I hear in a place "buried deep so deep"? Maybe I am listening to Mother Earth's heartbeat or the pulse of a caterpillar or an anthill reopening for the season. Maybe the heart of a seed is all ears and I can hear the songs of pre-hatched chicks, of groundhogs preparing to stretch after hibernation, of flowers still in the buds on branch tips and frost melting in early morning. If I attempt to make the sound that is at the heart of a seed for me, perhaps all that I would wish to produce is the reverent hush around a luxuriously lulled baby that no one ought to awaken prematurely.

So, to deepen the dimension of my understanding, I could choose to sculpt or fashion in clay a form that incorporates what I know so far in word, image, movement and sound. Or I may highlight just one aspect that somehow speaks to me. Perhaps I wax metaphorical and I mold the planet Earth the size of a baseball with a quarter section sliced out to expose the layers of the Earth's crust. Tucked under the Earth's mantle is an oval seed with a face the size of a peanut, with sleepy eyes and arms folded beside one cheek "fast asleep," dreaming of greener times. Well, maybe I am completely enthralled with the nested and contained feeling, so I form a set of nested bowls that are heart shaped, the smallest of which measures the amount in a teaspoon. Still, I could shape a clam shell the size of the palm of my hand, mostly shut but with just a hairline slit to shed a ray of light on the pearl sized seed heart within and contemplate that treasured, guarded place.

The possibilities range as far as human creativity will carry, but the shared understanding that develops from witnessing the way others explore the same concept can enlighten and enrich our own experiences in immeasurable yet tangible ways as they offer new dimensions to our sensory ways of knowing. Then, in knowing this poem, we not only memorize words, but we learn how to tap into nurtured feelings of groundedness, centeredness, and protectedness to invoke at times that we feel unsupported, scattered or exposed.

Camp Courageous is a grief camp created for children who are often the "hidden mourners" in families. Lost in the shuffling sea of medical decisions, funeral arrangements, and disputed wills, there has frequently not been space to check-in on the children's feelings about loss and death.

Some kids were so sophisticated as to think they were supposed to be fine, be good, not cry, and certainly not to make more trouble during this difficult time. Some came from families where the culture did not permit dwelling on anything that no one had the power to change. Others had families where the adults were so involved with their own loss of a child, parent, spouse, or sibling, they forgot that the children also had lost a significant relationship. The children were grieving in ways that were just as profound as adult losses. The children's losses should not be minimized and they should not be treated as if they are too young or too simple to understand or feel real pain.

Given such backdrops of non-communication about feelings, it was vital for the Camp Courageous to offer methods other than direct talk therapy to allow these children to process their grief. For several years I was graced to be the facilitator in the mask making art therapy process designed to help the children explore their emotions and share the feelings they had about the death of someone in their family. I had to make certain that the directives given were open enough and the art room space was safe enough to grant permission for the children to express any type of emotion that emerged in their grief process. The array of emotions the children were able to access from within themselves and depict outside of themselves on what once was a pile of blank-faced masks gave testimony to the power of the grief they were experiencing. When they allowed others to witness their emotions as they spoke about or shared with the group their individual feelings masks, their individual truths began the collective healing.

The artwork presented here is used by permission of Camp Courageous, a collaboration between Connections Individual and Family Services and Hope Hospice of New Braunfels, TX.

The mask to the far left displays a face aflame with anger that a father did not take good enough care of his health to last until a child's 8th grade graduation. The middle mask shows an attempt to soften with feathers the rage still present in hot red and orange. The rightmost face is full of the blueness of a child whose parent, grandparent and sibling all died of cancer in less than 2 years.

One summer I participated in an Expressive Therapy Expo at Pratt Institute in Brooklyn, NY. The first featured therapeutic process was in mask making. There were several artists who exhibited their process work. One had created in miniature an entire office setting which suggested that her whole persona at the office was a shell of sorts, projecting a certain urban, sleek and modern outer image while secretly longing for an old fashioned country life. Three other artists explored in more depth the world behind the masks, the core hidden within the shell. One work looked like a shoe box, generic except for the bold label AVERAGE EXTERIOR across the lid. A glimpse inside the box (which was set at an angle so it could not fully shut) revealed a colorful world within like a lush rain forest inhabited by vibrant flora and fauna. This sketch and poem is an artistic response to the theme **The Inner Mask: The Face Only I See**.

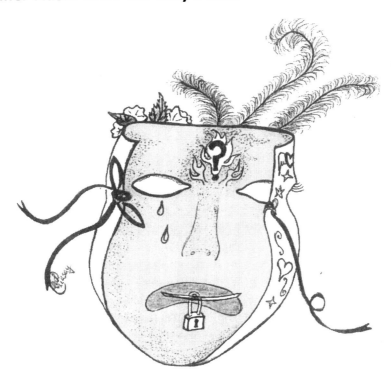

I don't know if I can ask you
all the burning questions that arise
or tell you just how hot and salty
loom the tears behind my eyes.
Dare I unlock the secret
to the pout guarded by toothy grin
so decorated with flowers and feathers?
Can I trust to let you in?
And if I shared even a sliver
of the inner me I never show,
If you could see, touch, hear, my mask's true face
would you even care to know?

All too often, I hear these unspoken questions from people who feel compelled to wear false masks, locked in rigid ways of being or driven to hide behind an image, trapped by the limits of what those around them could envision. These people could well be the seedings that never had sufficient substrate for them to emerge healthily from their shells. Their roots were not encouraged by the optimum warm/wet balance to which they learned to cling, to hold back, to spread themselves thin chasing whatever outside source they thought would help them thrive. There are others whose initial sprouting place was comfortable and supportive enough, yet as young plants they faced competition for sunlight and nutrients with other dominant or aggressive species that choked or overshadowed them. They could not retreat to their original shells but they developed new defenses that helped them survive.

At the Evangelical Ecumenical Women's Caucus (EEWC) of July 2006, there were many brave and accomplished women who told stories about some of the defenses females have to develop to survive in male dominated cultures. They spoke of women who wrote great poetry and literature under ambiguous or masculine pen names to mask their gender at time when "women did not write" or, to be more precise, only male writers were respected. They told of women who left churches because their call to preach, reconcile, or minister was unrecognized in patriarchal traditions. They described women who doubted their midwives' wisdom in the healing arts because it did not match the book knowledge of a scientific era. They honored women who courageously taught and passed on their knowledge nonetheless: women who realized they were formed in the image of the Creator and raised others' consciousness to see they were not inferior, flawed, or disfavored in any way.

The opposition we face chronically can dishearten us and influence us to form defensive masks. We can grow cramped behind walls of fear and anger over limits others impose upon us. Learning that we need not only live reactively is a way of letting down the guard mask and building a path to personal peace, a method of breaking from a shell that has become beyond protective but intolerably confining and risking transformation not by seeking retaliation but authenticity. Daring to find the freedom to be one's true self takes the courage to examine within and then stretch outward into new growing space. So many words this may seem, but the wisdom sinks in more by waves like the lyrics of the mantra sung at the EEWC following each key speaker:

As a seed before it grows
must be broken in the ground
so must we break from our shells
before we grow again.

As part of a reflection on the scriptural theme from Ephesians, "Rooted in love, empowered by God", each EEWC participant was given a seed: a pinto bean wrapped in a dark colored paper, soaked in water and sealed in plastic bag. They were instructed to tape the seed bag to the window and to watch for signs of growth during the conference. Throughout each day, the feedback on this reflection fed us all with new insights. One woman observed that the first to push its way through the softened skin of the seed was a root structure that eventually branched out into a network of hair-like, absorbent extensions. Someone with a masters degree in biology mentioned that first rooting structure is called a "radicle". We all seemed to know a lot of these radicals in pioneering human form. Another teacher pointed out that as the first green stem begins to uncurl that it carries up with it the split halves of the inner seed which give way to the first delicate leaves. So must we learn to carry forward that which nourishes us and shed that which no longer serves a purpose for our growth. We marveled that millennia before the installation of global positioning systems, each seed was equipped to know which way to root down and which way to lift leaves up.

What worlds of good we could do ourselves to reverently turn within and listen to the wisdom in the heart song of our souls.

Chapter 10
The Healing Power of Music
by Dana Clark

I believe music is magic.
I believe music is medicine.
I believe music can work miracles.
I believe music can help us remake the world.

In the small black and white photograph a year old baby wearing overalls sits in a high chair pulled up to an old piano. Her back is straight, her hands on the keys in proper position. The angle of her head indicates that she is watching her fingers make music. She is completely absorbed, oblivious to the rest of the world. On the music rack in front of her is a piece of sheet music, "Black and White Rag."

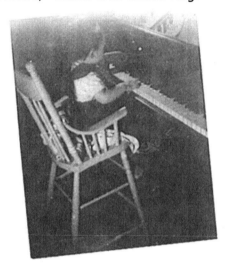

GIVE IT A TRY

Music is the language of emotion. When nothing else can quite express what you're feeling, music will. Collect recordings that touch your heart. Go for stylistic variety. Choose songs that evoke strong feelings of joy, rage, strength, fear, sadness, tenderness, love, etc. Keep them handy in a private listening spot. Use them as medicine, as often as needed. Listen to them. Sing along (at the top of your lungs, if need be.) Dance to them. Give yourself permission to laugh or cry. Repeat until you feel comforted. If you play an instrument or sing, develop a repertoire of favorite songs that portray a wide range of emotions. Turn to this outlet whenever you need it. Express yourself fully! Your own music will develop rich nuances of emotion if you play when you need to channel a powerful feeling. These songs can then be shared with others who need to hear them for their own healing.

Though the photo is black and white, I clearly remember that the high chair gleamed with shiny blue paint. The sheet music for "Black and White Rag" is still one of my treasured possessions. Looking at the photo, I realize that my lifelong fascination with the auditory art of music has long roots stretching back into my infancy, and it is too late to stop now! No wonder my identity was always bound up with the art of creating music. No wonder the most important decisions in my life were made in service to my musical evolution. It seems that I have always been willing to sacrifice anything for the sake of pursuing the musical adventure wherever it might lead. Some of those sacrifices were painful. Music was my greatest comfort. Music saved my sanity. Writing songs has saved my life.

Coping with the emotional turbulence of adolescence was no easy task in a small farm town with few alternatives. I learned there were two sources of relief: longs walks that brought me the mindless peace associated with physical exhaustion, and the catharsis of playing into the piano every nuance of the powerful emotions that at times seemed to be tearing me apart. Beethoven was very therapeutic, though I'm sure my interpretations were histrionic at times! As a teenager alone with my instruments and my emotional turmoil, the necessity of finding musical release provided a period of intense training that taught me to channel emotion through my fingers and voice.

As I had always planned, I enrolled as a music major when I entered college. As part of the curriculum, I had private lessons with one of my professors. He taught me only one thing: that I could never be a musician. He indicated that my technique was appalling, my sight-reading abominable, my repertoire inadequate. Rather than an expression of the heart, music became a mechanical exercise. Just like the little kids who give up singing for life once they've been told to stand in the back of the class and silently move their lips, the rejection of one teacher changed the direction of my life. I decided that if I couldn't be a musician, I would do something almost as important: I would try to save the world. I thought I could help others by studying psychology and working with children. For the next seven years I did just that, acquiring a B.A. in Child Psychology, and an M.A. in Behavior Modification. Music remained my "hobby." Accompanied by my guitar, I sang the folk songs of the day.

> **GIVE IT A TRY**
> Teachers can be invaluable at spurring your musical development. However—all music teachers are not created equal! Look for one who is willing to teach you what you want to learn in the way you need to learn it. Teachers who have a "one size fits all" approach may make you feel that their failure to meet your needs is your fault! Not true! There are as many ways to learn music as there are people on the planet. All ways are valid.

While working on my PhD in Educational Psychology I made friends with someone in that department who had played guitar in a rock band to help pay his way through college. We got together with our instruments and "jammed." When I discovered that my skills were just as good as his, I suddenly realized that if he could be a musician, so could I! In that moment my life reversed direction. A few months later I was playing in my first band, having dropped out of school and quit my job as a counselor. I was penniless and I was happy. When the band proved short-lived, I began writing songs and gigging solo, first in southern Illinois and later in Chicago, where there seemed to be no end of jobs for the working musician.

GIVE IT A TRY

Finding others with whom to share music making can be an opportunity for growth. Don't worry—your life probably will not change as radically as mine did! Invite others to your home for a sing-along. Host a get-together at which everyone is invited to bring their favorite recording to share. Find out about "picking parties" in your area. Be aware of the people in your circle of friends who play an instrument or sing, and do some casual music making with one or two at a time. Take advantage of opportunities to join in Christmas caroling groups, community choirs, music making at church, and drum circles.

My family was horrified that I had given up the security of my job and dropped out of graduate school to play in a rock and roll band. My life partner and I split up after being together seven years. I had difficulty explaining why these things were happening, even to myself! What gave music so much power over me? I couldn't claim that it was as essential to human survival as food and shelter, and yet I found myself willing to sacrifice everything in order to pursue it as my life's work. Through observation and reading I eventually came to understand how music affects individuals, bonding us to each other and to our community. Not mere entertainment, music exists in every culture and is commonly linked with spirituality and community. We are all inherently music-making creatures, and by participating in music we can all become more fully human.

I believe that music is nothing less than the first language of every human being. In the womb we grow familiar with the cadences of our mother's heartbeat, breathing, and movement. Though unequipped to understand the meaning of her words, we absorb the melody of her speech. From that moment in our prenatal development when our auditory nerves conduct the first signal, we hear the variations in pitch and tempo of our mother's voice associated with the physiological components of her emotional states. Blood of her blood, flesh of her flesh, we learn the meaning of her body music.

This communication becomes a duet at the moment of birth. Before speech develops, a mother must interpret the "musical" qualities of her infant's vocalizations in order to determine its needs. Attentive parents quickly learn the difference between the sound of a baby's cry of pain and the whine of fatigue, and are thereby guided in their responses.

GIVE IT A TRY

Feeling foggy and unfocussed? Need to be alert for a creative task? Let music help activate your brain! You can use recorded music, play your instrument, or sing. Focus all your attention on what you hear. Close your eyes. Music can be described as patterned sound. Keep track of the patterns you hear. Use your imagination to "see the sound" as patterns of shapes. Focus on one instrument, then another. Move your body and breathe in rhythm. Be open to the memories or fantasies that appear in your imagination. Your mental functioning should be quite improved after a few minutes!

If this ability to respond to musical elements is important to human survival, one would expect it to be something all humans share— something "hard-wired" in the human brain. With the functional brain imagery that allows scientists to examine which parts of the living brain are active, it has been found that as people listen to or participate in music, many different locations in the brain begin to work together in a coordinated fashion. At the very least, reading a piece of sheet music while singing and playing the piano requires that an individual use the parts of the brain associated with vision, hearing, memory, language, conscious breathing, and motor movements. Other activities may activate only a limited portion of the brain, whereas music "turns us on" more completely. In a way, we are never more whole, more completely ourselves than when we are listening or participating in music. Is this the reason music can make us feel so alive, centered, and transformed? Could this be the reason why a thought can become so much more powerful and easily understood when expressed as a lyric accompanied by music? With so many different locations in the brain involved in the processing, perhaps we understand the thought from many perspectives rather than from just one. The special joy I find while playing music rarely happens in any other way.

In a way, the discipline of playing music is akin to meditation, with the addition of serious consequences for losing focus! In meditation

> **GIVE IT A TRY**
>
> Before meditating, try chanting, singing, or playing an instrument to enhance your focus. During your meditation, try listening to the recorded music of Shakuhachi flute, a Japanese bamboo flute associated with Zen meditation.

there are no immediate negative effects when my mind wanders. In performance, when a distracting thought occurs to pull my attention away from my playing, my rhythm falters and discordant notes destroy my pleasure. Few activities have these kinds of negative consequences that serve to enforce careful attention to the present moment. During an intense performance, my attention can become so focused on the music that I lose my awareness of anything but the sound.

Afterward, as I return to everyday consciousness, I gradually become aware of details, like my name and what planet I'm on! I remember I have children. Because it takes me awhile to return to normal, it is not uncommon for me to get lost while driving home after a gig.

I spent nine years in the Chicago area, performing at clubs, coffeehouses, colleges, and hotels—anywhere people would listen to my music. It was in Chicago that I recorded my first album of original songs. I continued to study piano with private teachers, blues pianist Erwin Helfer and jazz teacher Skip Green. They had a flexible approach that gave me the tools I needed to pursue my own direction. The foundation they provided was so thorough that it continues to fuel my evolution today.

Supporting myself as a singer-songwriter in the big city took a great toll on my personal life. Those I cared about were sometimes negatively impacted by my decision to keep music my first priority. Music continued to remain my greatest source of comfort, but it is also true that it was often the cause of my pain. Eventually I became aware that audiences seemed to love me best when my heart was broken. The emotional power of my performance was strongest when my life was falling apart and I felt like there was nothing to cling to but the next song. Faced with the necessity of reconstructing my life from the ground up after a disastrous relationship, I jumped at the first gig that presented itself—playing a grand piano in a hotel lobby fifteen stories high near O'Hare Airport. The acoustics were phenomenal. Every syllable I sang echoed back from all fifteen stories, and my voice felt enormous, my intense emotional investment in each song magnified a thousand times. Best of all, the job was five hours a night, five nights a week. No other kind of therapy could have been so effective. I might wobble into work feeling traumatized and fragile, but I could always sing my way to strength and peace before the night was out. The hotel management loved me! I began to heal rapidly. My life seemed once more on track. Once again, a serious personal problem seemed to have a musical solution.

This song describes the process of putting life back together after personal tragedy.

You Resurrect Yourself
Copyright 1997 Dana Clark

No one seems to see your pain. You're too ashamed to ask for help
Sometimes you think you are to blame.
There's no one you can trust to tell
Despairing and defeated, a victim with no voice
Then just when you've lost your last hope, you find you have a choice

CHORUS: Then you resurrect yourself from the ashes of your dreams
You slowly work a miracle, though it's harder than it seems
Patiently you seek a way to restore your battered soul
You claim the fragments of your life. You learn to take control
Once you were broken
Now you're whole

Your sorrow strips you to the bone and leaves your naked heart to mourn
You struggle hard to stand alone, you labor long to be reborn
For each burden that you carry you must climb ever higher
Your spirit stronger since it has been tempered by the fire

CHORUS: As you resurrect yourself.....

Against all odds your scars have healed
and you've remembered how to laugh
What you have won you'll never yield, a champion in your own behalf
Your goals grow ever clearer. Your mind seems twice alive
You're empowered knowing you can face the worst and you'll survive

CHORUS: For you resurrect yourself from the ashes of your dreams
You slowly work a miracle and it's harder than it seems
Patiently you seek a way to restore your battered soul
You claim the fragments of your life. You learn to take control
Once you were broken
Now you're whole

As I healed, the job began to seem routine. My performance must have lost its sparkle, because eventually I was fired! I learned an important lesson about the boundary between professionalism and self-therapy, and my next gigs lasted as long as I wanted them. At the time I became pregnant with my daughter, I was working between five and seven nights a week. I continued to do so until I was five months pregnant and felt as big as a whale! In an effort to "get normal," before the baby arrived, my husband and I moved to San Antonio where he took a day job. I had thought that I would go back to playing when Annie was a few weeks old, but found it impossible to leave my baby. The recent move had left me with no local support network of family or friends. I decided to begin teaching piano at home, grateful that music was flexible enough to support my life even when my situation had changed radically. Putting Annie in her stroller, I walked the neighborhood, leaving fliers advertising my services on doorsteps. With a few satisfied customers, word of mouth advertising brought me more. When my son was born two and a half years later, I had twice as many reasons to continue combining music teaching with mothering. Determined to be the music teacher I wish I'd had, I never allowed myself to discourage a student. Though most of them might not be destined for the concert stage, I felt dedicated to the task of helping them all to experience the joy and personal growth of making music. My background in psychology helped me recognize the kind of music that fueled each individual's passion, and enabled me to present the material according to the student's learning style.

GIVE IT A TRY

Even if you have had no previous music instruction, IT IS NOT TOO LATE!!! Remember: Music was your first language. As long as you are breathing, you are a singer. As long as your heart is beating, you have rhythm. Many people believe that if they did not learn as children, they will not be able to learn as adults. Adults learn differently from children, but that difference can lead to rapid acquisition of skills. Children must learn everything in a concrete fashion, one building block at a time. Adults can learn conceptually, grasping an abstract concept and then applying it to many situations, causing a simple skill learned in one context to generalize broadly. I have found that with a few simple guidelines most adults can learn to improvise beautiful, expressive piano music in an hour, even with no previous experience.

If you have had disappointing experiences with a music teacher before, perhaps the problem was a poor fit between that person's style and your own. Music is often presented in an intellectual, abstract way that makes learning more difficult than it has to be. It should be as easy as for you as it was to learn your primary language. While reading music can be an important skill, music is an auditory art, not a visual art! Some people learn best by ear, and some of the best musicians I have ever played with do not read music.

One adult student who had never had any previous music experience confessed to me after several months of piano lessons that he had begun having a number of new insights in which he perceived important parallels between things he had previously thought were unrelated. Remembering how music stimulates and coordinates multiple brain sites, I exclaimed to him that his new insights were coming about because different parts of his brain were just now meeting for the very first time! I warned him that eventually he might end up becoming a philosopher, or trade his conservative lifestyle for something more adventurous!

Many students continue to study with me for years. I watch their lives change as music becomes part of them. Over the years I have learned that there is no one who cannot make music. I have had students with a wide range of learning disabilities and even congenital physical problems. The success they have experienced with music has generalized to other areas of their lives. They develop confidence that they can learn whatever they want. Adults who hadn't known they could carry a tune find their singing voices, learn to express themselves, and become empowered enough to take on other challenges in their lives. Children improve their grades in school because the discipline of coordinating so many different areas of their brain improves their ability to think. Children who learn to play expressively have an outlet that can help with the emotional challenges of adolescence. I believe that once they are exposed to the "natural high" of music making, they have an alternative to the street drugs they may encounter as teens.

Some of my students have suffered from depression. Sitting beside them at the piano, I have had the opportunity to watch from a front row seat as music does its healing work. A recently widowed older woman came back to life as she learned how to play piano the way she'd always wanted. Her energy

GIVE IT A TRY

Mood and behavior can be greatly influenced by music. Find a song that encourages your personal growth, and listen to it frequently. Think of it as "medicine." Learn to sing it. Make it your theme song— part of the soundtrack of your life. Paste the lyrics on your bathroom mirror. Soon you will find it playing on your "internal radio" like one of those advertising jingles that get stuck in your head. The song will continue to work its magic as you go through your day, whether you are consciously aware of it or not, encouraging you to make healthy changes in your life. When the song begins to lose its power, find a new one to take its place. Search out songwriters whose music revolves around the themes you need.

might have seemed low at the beginning of a lesson, but as we worked her mood would lighten, and she would leave proclaiming that what she had learned was "exciting!" I knew she was back on her feet when her life became too busy to continue lessons!

Many of my musician friends who play in nursing homes have told me that elderly people who are usually non-responsive can become animated and even sing lyrics perfectly even though they can no longer speak! They seem to "wake up," remaining alert for a period even after the music ends. It's true that "you can't take it with you when you go." This applies to music as well, but the songs that you learn may stay with you longer than anything else in life. They may provide others with a way of interacting with you after all other ways are gone.

The song below was written for a friend whose life seemed to fall apart unexpectedly. I have since found it very helpful when I need to encourage myself! It is a reminder to follow the still small voice inside as it leads us forward. The more we listen to that voice, the stronger it grows.

Trust Your Heart to Lead You Home
Copyright 1998 Dana Clark

When you began this journey you were sure how it would end
So you found the faith to follow though the road would often bend
But now you've lost direction. There's nowhere you can turn.
And from this crossroad all you see are bridges you have burned.

CH: Trust your heart to lead you home.
Find a path that's yours alone.
Listen to the voice inside you. It will grow in strength to guide you.
Trust your heart to lead you home.

Home is not the place you started from. It's a place you're reaching for
When you stretch beyond yourself to find a harbor in the storm.
A dream will be your compass. Your passion is your guide.
Sometimes you will have to crawl, but sometimes you can fly.

Like a painter with her canvas or a sculptor with his clay,
Your life takes shape beneath your hands as you work through each day.
You create a fabric with the threads of love you hold.
A tapestry of memory to warm you when you're cold

CH: Trust your heart to lead you home.
Find a path that's yours alone.
Listen to the voice inside you. It will grow in strength to guide you.
Trust your heart to lead you home.

I continued to teach music at home when my children reached school age. We homeschooled until my daughter was ready to enter high school. At this time, they seemed more independent from me and I was able to consider my own happiness. For my children as well as for myself, I was forced to admit that I needed to end my marriage and make a healthier life for the three of us. Again, it was music that provided me with a lifeboat. I began working as a substitute teacher at Circle School, and soon was hired there full time as Lead Teacher and Music Teacher. I became more involved in playing for services at my church and writing songs to fit the sermons. Later, I taught music classes for a homeschool organization, while taking on more private students.

For the last five years I have been Music Director at the Unity Church of San Antonio. I have had the opportunity to write songs for the services, many of which are about personal healing and transformation. Writing about serious subjects forces me to think deeply about what is true for me. I very much appreciate the challenge, and the songs that result are some of the ones I value most. For the most part, I try to avoid using religious language, since that can sometimes close minds against the message. Instead my aim is to focus on what is universally true about spiritual experience. This makes it possible for the songs to be useful in a wide range of performance situations.

> **GIVE IT A TRY**
>
> You can write songs! Write about changes in your life that you are trying to understand. As you write you will have the opportunity to discover what you really feel about your subject. We all have a unique perspective and a valuable message to express. Putting your bit of truth in a song turns it into something that can be shared. There are books in your local library that will give you practical guidelines about how to approach songwriting.
>
> You can find songwriting seminars on the internet. For an easy start, take a song you are familiar with and rewrite the words. After you are happy with the words, change the melody. There you have it—a brand new song!

Experienced musicians who play together frequently become so attuned to each other that it begins to seem as though they are communicating telepathically! Because music is a language of emotion, a rare intimacy and a powerful bond can develop. This is especially true when the musicians are involved in a romantic relationship! Many musicians end up with life partners who are also musicians. Eventually I came to realize that I would only be able to maintain an intimate relationship with someone whose life revolved around music as mine did. Who else would be able to understand why I could put everything on hold while finishing a song or a recording project? Who else could share my passion and my obsession? For the last eight years I have been blessed to share my life, songwriting, performing, teaching and recording with my husband Kevin Lewis. He is one of the finest guitar and bass players I have ever known. It is the best of all worlds to have the person I love join me in the work I love. Movies are fun. Walks are fun. Getting together with friends is fun, but our idea of the perfect date is going out to play music! Besides providing us with the greatest pleasure, it is no surprise that music gives us the opportunity to heal whatever may be wrong between us. We have found that everyday frustrations melt away as we work together to create the music neither of us could create alone. Judging from the way our names fit together, maybe it was always meant to be. It was no great feat of imagination to turn "Kevin Lewis" and "Dana Clark" into our band name: The Lewis and Clark (Musical) Expedition.

GIVE IT A TRY

Remember the old adage, "The family that prays together, stays together?" It can be equally true that "The family that PLAYS together, stays together!" Try incorporating musical projects in your family's activities. At my sister's Thanksgiving dinner not only did guests bring food to share, but most brought some sort of musical instrument as well. Together they discovered what kind of musical pot-luck they could create when everyone contributed what they could. Even instruments long-neglected were dusted off, and they sang together. Empty five-gallon water jugs make excellent drums, and simple shakers can be made with soda cans filled with dried beans or rice. As you create music together in a relaxed environment the rapport that develops with your loved ones can help as you work through stresses that arise in other areas. Best of all, you are making memories together that will return every time you hear one of the songs you have played. I treasure the memory of singing with my daughter Annie, whose voice is so similar to mine that it sounds like I am singing with myself. And it was very special to have Caleb join us onstage one evening to play bass on a song that I'm sure he learned in utero, as I often played it when I was pregnant with him!

A good alternative is to attend live music events with your loved ones. What is the most important difference between listening to recorded music and listening to live music? The recording doesn't know you're there! A live performer's show is greatly affected by the audience. An attentive, responsive audience brings out the very best the musician has to offer. The children in your family may be inspired to learn music after attending a performance. Assure them they can learn to do anything they want to learn. Assure yourself of the same thing!

GIVE IT A TRY

Each new instrument you learn is easier. By the time you get to three instruments, the rest seem like a snap! Every new instrument provides a different perspective that enables you to play your first instrument better. Take a chance! If you've played guitar all your life, learn something about piano. If you've always been a singer, try learning guitar. Your opportunities and progress will be enhanced. You will find new inspiration in old musical activities that might have become routine.

A visit to a music store can open a door to a new direction. Walk in and look around. Allow instruments to call to you. Take your time. BROWSE! Touch them. Discover the sounds in them. Take the attitude that you are there to discover which instrument will be your new best friend. There are many that are quite inexpensive. Many will encourage you to find the music in them even with no instruction. Check out penny whistles, recorders, ukeleles, harmonicas, dulcimers, guitars, glockenspiels, strumsticks (a very simple guitar-like instrument), thumb pianos, boomwhackers, drums and all the "percussion toys:" drums, tambourines, scrapers and shakers of every kind. (There's a reason they are called "toys!") Inexpensive keyboard instruments with built in speakers come with a wide variety of voices and built in rhythm tracks that can provide the basis for endless improvisation. Pick up a book as a guide, or get a music instruction DVD. Take home the instrument and experiment. Look up playing tips for that instrument on the internet. Something like a recorder or harmonica can be kept in your car so you can take advantage of unexpected time to play.

I have always loved singing. Piano was my first instrument. I began playing flute in the school band when I was nine. While in high school I learned to play guitar. In recent years, following my own advice that it is never too late, I have begun learning other instruments. I discovered that once you play one kind of flute, the rest are easy. Mandolin has been a joy, and saxophone is my newest passion.

Giving up the practice of psychology did not mean giving up my ambition to help others. Driven by my double passions of music and saving the world, it is no wonder that I eventually found myself trying to save the world with music! My life has become richer as I volunteer to play for causes related to social justice and peace. Each involvement of this kind has inspired the writing of new songs. Music with message and the purpose of creating a better world has power in it! Music performed with conviction can transform listeners, opening hearts to the possibility of change. I have been privileged to work with wonderful partners to organize community events to increase awareness of issues and raise funds to benefit agencies that work to improve conditions.

This song was written to promote awareness of domestic violence, and to help others recognize when they are involved in an abusive relationship.

The Pleasure of My Pain
Copyright 2003 Dana Clark

He didn't mean to hurt me. He's under so much stress.
And then the kids disturbed him when he tried to get some rest.
He doesn't mean the things he says; he speaks before he thinks.
I'm really not afraid of him, unless he starts to drink.
There must be something wrong with me—that's why he complains.
I know he loves me. How could he find pleasure in my pain?
I know he loves me. How could he find pleasure in my pain?

Some days it seems like everything I say or do is wrong.
I try to keep things quiet, and I try to get along.
But every time he needs to win, he makes sure that I lose.
I give him what he wants. It's so much worse if I refuse.
I make excuses for him, but I live my life in chains.
And I'm starting to suspect he must find pleasure in my pain.
I'm starting to suspect he must find pleasure in my pain.

I work to make him happy, but it's to no avail,
For he works even harder to make certain that I fail.
I'm ready to admit I might be better off alone,
But does that really matter when my children need a home?
My family says I shouldn't leave, but how can I remain?
Now I know that he's addicted to the pleasure of my pain.
I know that he's addicted to the pleasure of my pain.

I've found a safe place we can go. I know what I must do.
I've set aside some money, and my friends will help me, too.
He always told me if I left him I would not survive,
But now the kids are older. I know somehow we'll get by.
Then he won't hurt me anymore and I won't be ashamed.
For no one has a right to the pleasure of my pain.
No one has a right to the pleasure of my pain.

Powerful music has been at the heart of every important social movement. Music opens hearts and minds to new ideas, unifies people in common endeavors, and motivates change. We need only remember the protest songs of the Anti-War Movement and the freedom songs of the Civil Rights Movement to know that the right music at the right time can express the deepest longings of an entire generation and galvanize them to action.

This song was written as our country considered going to war in Iraq.

World of Justice, World of Peace
Copyright 2003 Dana Clark

I want to give my children a world that's safe in every way.
But now the radio reports new dangers every day.
Within this world of war my only weapon is a song.
All alone I'm not strong enough to right what's wrong.

CHORUS: But if we walk hand in hand, and we work side by side,
If we join heart to heart 'til we see eye to eye,
Then all the dreams we dream will be reality,
In a world of justice, a world of peace.

Can we be sure of freedom when so many are not free?
Why do some have plenty while some live in poverty?
We grow so tired of the struggle because the problems never end.
But in each other's eyes we find the faith to try again.

CHORUS: For when we walk hand in hand...

Seven billion of us on a planet that's so small.
Someday we may realize we're family after all.
And when we reach out to heal each other, set each other free,
We'll find only sisters, brothers, not one enemy.

CH: Then we will walk hand in hand, and we'll work side by side.
We will join heart to heart 'til we see eye to eye.
Then all the dreams we dream will be reality,
In a world of justice, a world of peace.

A few years ago I worked with the San Antonio peaceCENTER and the Unity Church to promote events to bring awareness to *A Season for Nonviolence*. I produced two compilation CDs of music on the theme of peace. These were sold to raise funds for services for the people who were homeless and for children who were abused. Because I was

---

GIVE IT A TRY

Volunteer to serve in some way in a community effort that addresses a problem about which you feel a special concern. Look for ways music can be incorporated in that effort. Musical performances added to an informational event can bring in a bigger audience and allow the event to become a fundraiser, as people can be charged an admission price. Performers are sometimes willing to provide their services at a reduced fee for a worthy cause, especially if they are allowed to sell their CDs at the event

---

looking for a way to involve more people in the peace concerts we had planned, I invented the San Antonio Peace Choir. My goals were to be inclusive of everyone who had a heart for peace, regardless of musical experience, to minimize the time spent on preparation, and to maximize the impact on the community. In my advertising, I emphasized that singing in the Peace Choir was not about vocal technique, but rather about being willing to become an instrument for the music of peace to sing itself into the world. These were my guidelines:

1. If you are breathing, you have already passed the audition.
2. No experience is necessary, and you do not have to read music.
3. A single one-hour rehearsal is all that is required.
4. Singers could begin learning the music on-line at my website.

I held rehearsals at different times and locations during the month leading up to a concert. I passed out booklets of lyrics, and the music was learned by call and response in the oral tradition. I made a deliberate attempt to reach out to a wide variety of people in order to present a true rainbow of diversity. People were encouraged to bring family and friends to sing with them. No one was too young or too old. We had singers as young as four and as old as 82. At our first concert we had about 70 singers participating. At our second concert, we had about 140! A full band backed up the Choir: bass, drums, piano, and guitar. Soloists sang some parts of the songs. I rarely saw anyone glance at a lyric book. Instead, everyone sang from their hearts, faces glowing, expressing their true passion for a better world. The music unified us, creating a powerful vision, making us all believe that peace is possible.

At the beginning of a rehearsal I would notice some roughness in the blend of voices. Not everyone would be perfectly on pitch, and some voices were too loud. Slowly we learned the first few songs. About twenty minutes into a rehearsal I would suddenly realize that the voices sounded balanced, tuned, and very sweet. We could sing through a new chorus just once as call and response, and immediately sing it in perfect unison. It is part of the magic of music. I was reminded of the way fish school, and the way birds fly in perfect formations, all seeming to wheel and turn on cue.

Listening and making music together in community is an essential part of being human. We have lost much of that in today's world, where music is too often thought of as a commodity to be bought and sold. It is easy to get the feeling that only a few special people have talent; they become "stars" and no one else has anything to offer. Kevin and I strongly disagree with that idea! Part of our mission is to help others discover they have more music inside than they ever suspected. We do this as teachers with our music students. We do this as performers when we invite the audience to make the music with us.

Every Monday evening Kevin and I host a musical gathering where all are encouraged to participate. We work to break down the artificial barrier between audience and performer. Some of the finest musicians in the city have played for us, as well as some of the newest musicians in the city! All are honored for their contributions. It is our desire to provide an opportunity for the power of music to accomplish its very important work in the world: enriching our human experience by calling forth a subtle variety of emotions and promoting healing and transformation by helping us integrate body, mind, and spirit.

Many times I have seen musicians who have never met before, do not know each other's names, and do not necessarily speak the same language sit down with their instruments and on the spur of the moment create beautiful music together. How do they do this? By listening carefully to each other and being responsible about how they contribute the sound of their instruments to the overall composition. What if instead of sending our politicians to Washington (or to the United Nations) we sent our very best musicians. What if they first worked out harmonies with each other and improvised a symphony of new music to which they all contributed. Somehow I think tackling social/political issues after that would be much easier and more likely to result in justice and peace.

Music has been my greatest comfort. Music has saved my sanity. Writing songs has saved my life.

> I believe that music is magic.
> I believe that music is medicine.
> I believe music can work miracles.
> I believe that music can help us remake the world.

It is my hope for us all that we find the healing we need. I hope music helps you as much as it has helped me.

Hopeful Heart

Copyright 2007 Dana Clark and Kevin Lewis

A hopeful heart can change the blackest night to brightest light
A hopeful heart transforms our aching pain to pure delight
Even when our dreams have died, the world seems torn apart
Nothing can resist the power
Nothing can resist the power
Of a hopeful heart

I'm filled with gratefulness today for what tomorrow brings
Empowered now by hope I'm finding joy in everything
Despair has tried to tell me my faith cannot be restored
But blessings stand outside and knock
Blessings stand outside and knock
So hope opens the door

A hopeful heart
A hopeful heart
Nothing can resist the power
Of a hopeful heart

Yes, hope supplies a fearless faith that makes our dreams come true
Even when we face a choice and don't know what to do
A still small voice will guide us as we make a brand new start
For Spirit speaks most clearly
Spirit speaks most clearly
To a hopeful heart

When success seems out of reach and we're afraid to lose
We must come to see that we are always free to choose
To search for hints of sunshine though the clouds are all around
For the glass is half full and rising
The glass is half full and rising
Not half empty, going down

A hopeful heart
A hopeful heart
Spirit speaks most clearly
To a hopeful heart

Chapter 11
Healing Earth – Healing Ourselves

Michelle Balek, OSF

"In a study spearheaded by the Environmental Working Group (EWG) in collaboration with Commonweal, researchers at two major laboratories found an average of 200 industrial chemicals and pollutants in umbilical cord blood from 10 babies born in August and September of 2004 in U.S. hospitals. Tests revealed a total of 287 chemicals in the group. The umbilical cord blood of these 10 children, collected by Red Cross after the cord was cut, harbored pesticides, consumer product ingredients, and wastes from burning coal, gasoline, and garbage...

Of the 287 chemicals we detected in umbilical cord blood, we know that 180 cause cancer in humans or animals, 217 are toxic to the brain and nervous system, and 208 cause birth defects or abnormal development in animal tests."
    (See the Body Burden website for the complete report:
    http://archive.ewg.org/reports/bodyburden2/execsumm.php)

This report released in 2005 points out how intimately connected we are physically with our environment, and how pervasive our human footprint on all of creation really is. Our daily choices impact whether our environment will be a healthy one or not – not only for ourselves, but also for future generations.

A few years ago I was on a team giving a retreat on creation. We had devised a beautiful visual for the weekend: a sand box in the middle of the gathering space, complete with blooming flowers and natural colorful decorations. Participants seemed to like it, but didn't say much about it. Part way into the retreat, before one of the sessions, the team rearranged the box and its contents so the scene greeting the participants was a very different one: there was blackish oil in the water bowl, crumpled papers and wrappers were strewn about, flowers were knocked over...There was an audible gasp from many as they entered the space. For the first time many of them began to realize the heaviness weighing on them for the sin of humanity – their sin- in despoiling creation. They began to recognize the need for apologizing and asking forgiveness as they moved forward with a renewed commitment to cherish this Mother Earth, gift from the Creator.

Our health – physical, mental, emotional, spiritual – is intimately connected with the health of creation. Yet we often don't recognize this connection at all. Getting back in touch with creation helps us to get back in touch with ourselves. At different times in my life, I've lived close to Lake Erie and to Lake Michigan. At either place, I was amazed at how the lake before me was always the same, and yet was always changing – almost to match my moods. When my dad died, I remember walking along the shore of Lake Michigan and allowing the rhythmic sounds of the waves to wash over my soul and begin to soothe and heal my inner self from the tremendous loss I felt. My tears became part of the lake, and the lake, my tears. There was a gentle consistency of that sound that spoke of life continuing on through change.

Or there was the time I was "downsized" and was left rather
unceremoniously without work and I had such rage within me. It was an overcast and windy day, the lake was rather wild, and as I walked the lakeshore, fuming, I suddenly directly faced the lake and hollered out: "You are angry and so am I!" It swallowed my words in knowing acceptance, allowing me to begin to let go of an anger that was consuming me – and move on to live life again. Allowing myself to recognize aspects of creation not only helped me begin my healing process, but also affirmed my desire to preserve this beautiful creation.

> *Lie upon the earth and let Her absorb what is making you ill or what keeps you victimized.*
>
> *All energy can be transformed into healing energy*

Getting back to that study and the amount of physical pollution within our very bodies: how do we begin to make a difference in healing Earth and ourselves? The most important thing is to take ONE step and do it today. That one step will lead to another and another...and before long, you will discover yourself on a journey of conversion in lifestyle and life choices that are more sustainable and that lead to greater health for yourself and the planet.

My interest in creation and sustainability, and my belief that we are intimately connected to all creation, led me to pursue an MA in Sustainable Development. As I look at the world today, I see such disparities between nations and between people within nations. We are hoarding and wasting resources, destroying our environment and the lives of many people in the process. We are not being "smart" about how we grow our cities or meet our needs. Part of the problem is we have been convinced that our "wants" ARE our "needs" and feel they should be immediately satisfied, while ignoring the basic needs of the majority around the globe. We HAVE to rethink "development" and perhaps we here in the US need to become LESS "developed" so that others may simply live. Imposing our "way of life" on others has not worked and will not work, firstly, because we are using up Earth's resources at an alarming rate. The Global Footprint Network revealed on October 6, 2007 that that very day, October 6, was **Ecological Debt day** – the day when humanity has consumed all the resources the planet will produce this year. With Ecological Dept day falling on October 6th, our overshoot of the planet's resources is 30 percent. (http://www.insnet.org/ins_headlines.rxml?id=5129&photo=)

Secondly, imposing our "way of life" on others will not work because we are not honoring their uniqueness and dignity. I am haunted by a passage from an essay in the Development Dictionary on "Participation" by the development expert, Majid Rahnema:

> *"As a rule, the necessity for a spiritual dimension, and for a revival of the sacred in one's everyday relationships with the world, seems to be rediscovered as a basic factor for the regeneration of people's space. Wherever this spiritual dimension has been present, it has indeed, produced a staggering contagion of intelligence and creativity, much more conducive to people's collective 'efficiency' than any other conventional form of mass mobilization."*

What Rahnema is saying, is that the best kind of "development" –that *from the people themselves*- is happening in those places across the globe where people are allowed to rediscover the spiritual dimension in their lives, culture, world; where they are reviving these interconnections between humanity and the rest of creation, and approaching life more holistically. Development often implies a "lack" of something, a neediness, and that the "developed" world has all the answers for the "developing" world. Perhaps we have it backwards – and we in the "developed" world are the needy ones, lacking what we truly need to not merely survive but really live. There is much we can learn from our brothers and sisters who make up the majority on this planet.

Sustainability, simply put, is a "balance maintained over time." What do we need to balance? We should be looking at a triple bottom line: economic, equity in the social/political spheres, and environmental. We have to weigh the costs of our decisions not just in dollar amounts but also in the impacts to social capital as well as the environment. We have to ask the tough questions and be willing to sacrifice some comfort-complacency, in order to heal creation and ourselves.

Sustainability requires a more "communal" approach to life rather than the "rugged individualism" our culture enshrines as a god. Here are some ways to begin to live more sustainably, healing Earth and ourselves in the process:

- ❖ Join a Community Supported Agriculture project near you
- ❖ Participate in the Smart Growth movement to curb urban sprawl
- ❖ Be wise about your water use
- ❖ Use mass transit, walk, bike, or car pool more
- ❖ Reduce, Reuse, Recycle
- ❖ Buy local – support local farmers
- ❖ Spend time sitting with creation, listen to what she teaches
- ❖ Make conscious choices, taking into account how they will effect the 7th generation
- ❖ Join a local/national group working on these issues to join your voice and efforts with others
- ❖ Invite family, friends, neighbors, co-workers to join you in these efforts

Listed below are some resources to help you along the journey. Take the first step toward healing Earth. Each successive step will be revealed as you unite your efforts with those of others in this process and discover the awe, wonder and important place of all God's creation in our common journey.

....

Shard, Philip Sutton; **The Healing Earth: Nature's Medicine for the Troubled Soul**, 1994; NorthWord Press, Minnetonka, MN

Durning, Alan Thein & Ryan, John C.; **STUFF: The Secret Lives of Everyday Things;** 1997; Northwest Environmental Watch, Seattle, WA

Carroll, John E.; **Sustainability and Spirituality**; 2004, State University of New York Press, Albany, NY

Yale Divinity School; ***Reflections: God's Green Earth***; Spring 2007, Vol 94, No. 1; New Haven, CT

Chapter 12
Spirituality and Inner Healing
WE ARE ONE

By Glee Miller, MTS, DD

"I am a Jew, a Muslim, a Hindu and a Christian."
Mahatma Ghandi

Beautiful words of truth spoken by a deeply spiritual man who gave his life for peace in his own country of India.

This chapter is not intended to be about how different we are in the expressions and spirituality of our diverse beliefs, but our sameness and how our inner depths are so connected to God, Allah, The Nameless One, Deva, The Great Spirit, The Holy One, YHWH. We are the same - brothers and sisters - created in love so that our love is our common denominator in promoting world peace and healing. I tell the stories from my own faith tradition, may you adapt the vocabulary to fit your own.

From the Christian Scripture Matthew 10:8, "The gift you have received, give as a gift." Called by God to be a minister, my vocation took shape as a hospital chaplain. My experience and blessing during these years, was that this inner city hospital brought to me many diverse people - dark, light, rich, poor, old and new - many different faiths. To see God's love work in the spiritual healing of many was to be a gift, a privilege and deep learning.

May I share.......

Sanjay

In a cardiac surgery unit, I stopped one morning to visit a gentleman from India, who was scheduled for heart surgery. He was lying on the bed, very stiff, with the covers pulled almost over his face. I asked him to tell me how he was. His reply came tentatively, "I'm ok." Taking a chance, I replied, "You don't look ok, this must be very scary for you." His demeanor shifted and, after a while he admitted that he was scared - most frightened that he would die and leave his wife and two children alone. We talked about fear of dying, what happens after death and how we are bound together by love. By the second visit, he welcomed me and asked how to talk to his wife about his fear but also about his love and concern for her and the boys. Sanjay, who was a medical professional and an admitted workaholic, was then able to speak to his wife about his fear of death and of his deep feelings for his family. This communication brought a new closeness to their marriage and he was able to face the surgery with peace.

Some days after his successful surgery and recovery, Sanjay shared with me that his life was completely changed and that he felt such peace that he planned to work less and move his priorities to his loved ones and also to renew the practice of his faith.

Mary

A call to the OB unit brought me in into see a young, heavy, black woman who was pregnant with twins and in premature labor. She was very friendly but not too sure what to do with a white, Catholic chaplain. However, it didn't take very long for us to become friends. She spoke about her anxiety concerning delivering her babies so prematurely that they might not live.

In the days of waiting, she spoke about her life as a prostitute. Over some days, she became more reflective of the impact of her chosen profession on her role as a mother and how that would affect her children. Her need to return to a church community surfaced in our visits and we prayed together as sisters for guidance.

Even with the very best care and an excellent obstetrician, twin baby girls were born prematurely, and too tiny to have full developed lungs, died minutes after birth. This mom was joyful as she held and bonded with her dying babies. She cried tears of joy at what miracles they were and how perfectly God has created each of them and, then, tears of sadness that she would have to bury them and they would never go home with their Mom.

In the following day or two, this Mom in mourning shared that even though she didn't understand why her babies died, she was sure that they were in Heaven and would be waiting for her when she got there. At one point, I asked her what message she thought her babies would have for her. She replied with a sweet, sad smile that they wanted her have a better life and return to school and no longer sell herself as a prostitute.

Did she do it? I don't know. What I do believe is that God was brought closer to her through the birth and death of precious babies and her life will never be the same again.

Julianne

Julianne, a young married woman, wife of a physician, came to speak with me in my office. The sadness in her beautiful face reflected her tale of sexual and physical abuse from her father. As she spoke, she shared that, over many years, she had been to priests, psychologists, psychiatrists and found no inner peace. Her request that morning was that I pray with her for inner healing. The following morning, a small chapel was our setting. In this quiet spot, I prayed: "Close your eyes and picture yourself as a little girl in your bedroom. You hear a knock at the door." Julianne immediately began to tremble with fear. I prayed quietly for God to surround her with peace until she was quiet again. Continuing, I prayed, "In your room you can feel the peace. You hear a knock at the door and a man begins to come in.It is not your father. Allow God to come over to you and give you a big hug. Just feel the healing presence move all through you touching all the fear, hate and hurt." Then I just sat with her and prayed silently. After a while, she begins to tell me what had happened during the prayer. Hearing the knock at the door, she began to panic because she thought it was her father. When she realized that it was Jesus, she was able to allow that Presence come over to her and hold her and that Jesus had told her not to worry, that her father would not hurt her anymore. She stated that she felt peace and love flow through her taking away the painful memories. By this time, her face was peaceful and smiling.

A week later Julianne returned to tell me that her fear was completely gone and she now felt compassion for her father. Some months later, she again returned to share that her father had cancer and that she had been able to go and care for him until he died. During his dying process, Julianne's father had asked her to forgive him and they were reconciled. Julianne's husband also telephoned me that his wife was so different after the prayer - no more depression or fear. He was most grateful. Now over 20 years have passed and Julianne remains healed, healthy and whole, living her life well.

Rachel

My encounter with a young Jewish woman was to be a time of learning for me. This young lady had flown from Israel to give birth to her child, who would be given to new adoptive parents. Rachel seemed wary of me at first, but as the days passed, she began to trust and tell me her story...

She was engaged to a young man of whom her parents approved. When Rachel became pregnant, the family responded by shaming her.

So an adoptive family was found in the United States and alone she came to give birth in a strange country, knowing no one. Her plan was to return to Israel after the baby was born and resume her life as if nothing had happened.

Rachel did not want to see the baby or give the baby a name. I shared with her my belief that God already has a name for each child and that God has a name for her child and that her baby already knew her as mother. She, at first, rejected these thoughts but became more reflective as the birth neared. Thankfully, her fiancé called daily to give her support, but no word came from her parents.

A beautiful, healthy baby boy was born, but Rachel refused to see or hold him. The adoptive parents were notified to come for the baby. I again spoke to Rachel of importance of bonding with her child, telling him her plan for his new life with new parents and having a prayer commending him to Yahweh's care.

The nurse called me to say that Rachel had requested a visit from me. She announced to me that she had decided to see her baby but she felt scared and did not know what to do or say. I reassured that I would be with her to help. Asking the nursery to bring the baby in, I took him and placed him in his mother's arms. Her first response was, "Oh, he's ugly. What do I do now?" I told her to talk to him and just tell him about daddy and grandparents. As she looked into the face of that baby, her face was transformed, her heart melted and she began to cuddle him and smile. I quietly departed the room for a while to allow the bonding to continue.

The adoptive parents were to come and pick up the baby the next day. We needed a plan. Rachel decided that she would like to have a goodbye prayer service, so we thought, prayed and planned.

The next morning, the nursery dressed the baby and he was brought to Mom. (I might add that the nursing staff was very apprehensive about this patient bonding and visiting with the baby so much.) But this time, Rachel was ready to receive baby David - the name she had chosen for him. Her first words as she took him in her arms were, "You're so beautiful." Her face was radiant. Just as we planned, I left the room as she told him about his "new" parents and why she had to give him up, that she would always love him and carry him in her heart. After a bit, I returned and we took photos of him. Her request was for a prayer that Yahweh would care for David and that his new parents would love him and care for him well. It was with great difficulty and tears that Rachel gave him back to me - never to be seen again by her. More tears...

Meanwhile, the adoptive parents had arrived. Rachel requested that I speak with them and then return to her with a report. *More* learning for this chaplain! As I introduced myself to a very nice, young couple, a pretty blonde and her husband, both Orthodox Jews, I tried to shake his hand. Big boo boo! The wife, seeing that I wasn't aware of their customs, quickly took my hand of greeting. (Jewish Orthodox men do not shake the hand of a woman.) They, too, were nervous about seeing their new baby. Would everything go right? Would the Mom change her mind? Seeing they were so sweet and gentle, I felt that I could give Rachel a "good report".

Later, back in Rachel's hospital room, when I described the adoptive couple to Rachel, she explained that the adoptive parents were Orthodox Jews who adhered very strictly to their beliefs. She seemed satisfied with my assessment of them and signed the adoption papers when the social worker came. I could see she was at peace.

Later, the adoptive couple and I went to the nursery to see their new son. Nervous and shaking, both cried tears of joy as they held their precious new baby.

Rachel returned to Israel carrying with her a memory box containing the blue outfit David had been wearing during their goodbye service, his arm band, his newborn hat and the photos, plus precious memories of her time with baby David ... memories that will never leave his Mother's heart. And for baby David, who would have loving new parents, the effects of receiving his Mother's love and affirmation was imprinted on his mind, heart and soul, allowing him to hold love and acceptance forever, thus healing what might have been a bitter, abandoned feeling affecting the remainder of his life. And I was left with a poignant memory, of Rachel singing a Jewish lullaby to her child as she said goodbye. Two lives forever changed and healed by the One Who Loves.

Me

God's call to me opened doors of love and learning. The common denominator of love is stated in the Christian Scripture in John 13:34 "Love one another, Such as my love has been for you, so must your love be for each other". My experience as a hospital chaplain and other life experiences have taught me that love reaches beyond the barriers that denominations have imposed. All of us were planned carefully with love and sent by our Creator to love one another, no ifs, ands or buts. Whether we are red, black, white, yellow, Jew, Muslim, Christian, Hindu or other, our connection to our God is the same - children of our Mother/Father God.

I believe that the process of inner healing connects us with our own deep sense of God that is forever present, helping us to be healed in spite of life's circumstances. Our physical bodies are created by God to reach out for healing, simply because our cells are created by God, thus containing God's love - always reaching back to our original creation. Because our deepest inner core, who is our Creator, cannot change, our own need for inner healing can be accessed again and again. With our Creator's love, all things are possible.

Chapter 13
Awakening
towards Inner Reliance and Bliss

Bismil'lahir-Rahmanir-Raheem
In the Name of Allah, The Most Gracious, The Most Merciful

By Narjis Pierre

May Allah SWT forgive any of my transgressions; all goodness is from Allah SWT, and from my self is all confusion…

I am a Muslim woman. I 'reverted' to Islam at the age of 29, and it was the best and most blessed one decision I could have made, though nothing did I know about Islam.

Immediately, this 'Deen' (specific way of living) gave me an outer framework to follow (*shari'a* – religious law) and purified me over the next couple of weeks and months from addictions to alcohol, cigarettes and societal peer-pressures.

Muslim men and women ideally attempt to use Prophet Muhammed (saw), and all previous Prophets, as role models and guides on their path towards Allah (SWT). All believers are encouraged to tread steadily on the 'prophetic path', which means following the *sunna'* (teachings and sayings) of the Prophets, which in no way can contradict anything revealed by Allah SWT.

The Prophet Muhammed (saw) (~570-632 C.E.) conducted himself 'perfectly' while he behaved and exemplified the best state of '*Iman*' (faith and trust in Allah SWT), Islam (perfecting the commanded rituals and being in a totally submitted state towards Allah SWT), and '*Ihsan*' (directing self and life towards beauty and excellence). He exhibited the best character because he was always in the 'presence' of Allah SWT, inwardly as well as outwardly.

A *hadith* says:
'He (Prophet Muhammed) worshipped Allah as if he saw Allah; and if he did not see Allah then he knew that Allah saw him.'

I was fortunate to be in the company of a Muslim community, which was living according to Islamic and religiously-oriented life transactions, whose intent was to allow the opportunity for each one to search and dig for deeper meanings into one's life and the purpose thereof. The community's goal was to practice the very best behavior and interactions in everyday life, living Islam.

Personally I have been and still am on a quest of growing in self-knowledge and my teacher has stayed stable in his teachings and interpretations of everything: I am a student of 'The Academy of Self-Knowledge - ASK <www.askonline.za> - an on-line interactive study course developed and overseen by Shaykh Fadhlalla-Haeri, in which he attempts to open for his students, windows toward understanding and knowledge of one's inner and spiritual journey.

What follows is my compiled reflection from the first lessons of this ASK course, which is open to anyone, regardless of faith tradition.

'The thing we tell of can never be found by seeking, yet only seekers find it.'

Bayazid Bistami, Muslim mystic
(died 874 after hijra)

<u>What it is, and why do we seek bliss?</u>

Bliss is the state of absolute harmony, with no ripples whatsoever to disturb peace, serenity and the condition of surrender.

Bliss embraces the whole human being: there is the physical, 'outer' component: there can be no bliss, if there are aching bones, tired muscles, tensions and the need to nourish the body. And there is the intellectual and spiritual, 'inner' component: being in a state of bliss, all thoughts have come to calm. The impact of arriving at a momentary state of bliss will be felt in the body, heart and soul.

Arabic abbreviations and words that will appear in the text:

Allah - Al-Lah – The One, besides which there is no other – God

Tawheed – the understanding of One-ness; everything created; the 'Seen' and the 'Unseen' are interconnected and all relates back to the Creator

Nafs' - self - derive from the arabic root 'nafas' which mean 'breath'

'Ruh' - spirit/Soul - echoes the Divine Breath

Abbreviations follow the mentioning of names with due respect:

SWT - *Subhana wa ta'Ala* = Glorified be Allah, the Highest

Saw - *sallalahu aleihi wa sallem* = peace and blessing be upon him (the Prophet(s) (pbuh)

Qur'an – Scripture, Recitation, Reading

Hadith – saying of Prophet Muhammed (saw)

Hadith Qudsi – revelation from Allah SWT, not collected in Qur'an but collected as a Divine Hadith

Asma al-Husna – Names or Attributes of Allah SWT – important source of reflection

Na'eem – bliss

Dhikr – Remembrance - vocal or silent repetition of words or phrases; constant vigilance of action and thought-control; constant in the focus on Allah SWT

We seek bliss, because that brief moment brings us into deep and complete stillness: we become tranquil, all the way deep into our body, mind and soul, and find our 'selves' absorbed by reflected Asma al-Husna, Attributes of Allah SWT such *as as-Salaam* - The Source of Peace; *al-Latif* – The Subtle; *ya Wadud* – oh All-Loving.

We yearn for and seek virtuous and 'elevated' components that mirror and echo the *Asma al-Husna*, Attributes of God.

To arrive at bliss within the context of this human entity, there must be an experience of moments of transcendence, where one frees oneself from the chains of physical torments and emotional blockages.

During such brief moments of 'peacefulness', as may become possible after times of intense love-devotion and forgiveness-begging, deep meditation and prayerfulness, we may get a faint 'tasting' or feeling of what bliss may be like.

Feeling bliss is very physical. Experiencing bliss puts all worries to rest and allows us to 'feel' a paradisiacal moment.

This state of stillness, spaciousness, light and joy cannot last, because we are living in the world of duality, and we must get back to 'living', back to the family, the work, the action...

> **'...to be in this world, but not of it...'**
> Shaykh Fadhlalla-Haeri

Being created by the Life-Giver, *Ya Hayy,* I become. I am.
And within 'I am' lies the whole spectrum of all possibilities, in either direction of goodness, righteousness and piety, or weakness and negative tendencies, i.e. 'sin'. Both these primordial forces of attraction and repulsion are necessary to complete my whole, and to allow me to come to understand 'tawheed' - One-ness – which in turn allows me to 'surrender' to The One with knowledge.

With my *himma*, desire tuned to 'heavenly' Unconditional Love, the force of attraction, goodness, healing, unifying and harmonizing is stronger and the more dominant force, by default, will constantly be available to me; once my mind and heart become tired of the 'piecemeal' earthly realities of my quest, it should do 'tawbah', - turning towards' and seek *Ya 'Ali* - The Highest. This is an on-going continual process.

Bliss is then, when the forces of attraction and repulsion silence, becomes less imbalanced and more manageable, as one now is better able to hold and absorb the tension of the opposites, and put oneself on the perfect balancing point, aimed towards *Ya Noor* – Light, and *Ya Wadud* - Love.

Towards Self-Reliance: Stages of the Self

Qur'an 41:53
'We will show them (humankind) Our (Allah's) signs on the horizons and within themselves, in order to make clear to them (humans), that Allah is indeed Truth.'

Prophet Muhammed (saw) was the chosen body for reception, memorization and dissemination of the message of the Wise Qur'an. With Allah SWT's Wisdom it proved to be the guidance to train and groom the Prophet Muhammed's (saw) character to perfection. He became known as 'Insan ul Kamil'– the 'perfect human being'.

The object of human's quest for knowledge of purpose of existence is to come to recognize Allah SWT and know the revealed commandments by the prophetic examples.

Hadith Qudsi:

**'Kuntu kanzan makhfiyan…
I (Allah SWT) was a Hidden Treasure,
and loved to be known,
so I created…'**

We come to know Allah SWT, Who created through Love, by recognizing, uncovering and learning about the outer, visible creation and what is within our own selves. Knowledge of the self opens doors to greater knowledge of Allah SWT.

**7 And the soul and its perfection! –
8 So Allah revealed to it (the soul) its way of evil and
its way of good.
9 s/he is indeed successful who causes it
(the soul) to grow
10 and s/he indeed fails who buries it.**

In Islam, the fundamental understanding is, that Allah SWT creates with Wisdom and All-Knowing, and because one of the many attributed Realities is *'al-Kaamil* - 'The Perfector', our faith has to necessarily believe, that God created everything in perfection:

'By the self/soul and Allah Who made it perfect'…
Qur'an 91:7

…by which Allah SWT confirms for us that we are born with inherent perfection, beckoning from the zone before time and space and from a Reality to which we all will return, the Hereafter, the Unseen. The *'Ruh'*, which Allah SWT 'breathes' into the physicality of the embryonic body (Qur'an 15:29), acts as a reflected carrier of celestial Light of Divine Consciousness. Hence, perception into Divine Mysteries is potentially already available to us when entering this earthly domain, this world of duality. But:

> **'Then Allah inspired it (the soul/self) to understand**
> **what is right and wrong with it.'** Qur'an 91:8

Subtle 'outer' influences on the *Ruh* begin to absorb as first ripples in the formative stage even in the womb, but in a 'big bang' fashion once life is born and breath is drawn, and a distinction is necessarily formed on the *nafs* (self-consciousness) and the *Ruh* (Soul-Consciousness): Soul-Consciousness will always retain and continue to recognize its original blueprint of heavenly purity, while 'self' will have to dabble through the different levels as are mentioned in Qur'an:

Tyrannical, animalistic self, Qur'an 12:53:
> **'The tyrannical self certainly impels to evil...'**

Regretful, self-reproaching self, Qur'an 75:2:
> **'I (Allah) call to witness the regretful self...'**

Inspired, contented self, Qur'an 91:7-10:
> **'By the self,**
> **And the proportion and order given to it;**
> **And its inspiration to its wrong and to its right...'**

Serene, peaceful self, Qur'an 89:27-30:
> **'O soul, in (complete) rest and satisfaction,**
> **Come back to thy Lord...'**

With maturity and improved understanding, self and Soul will engage inner and outer senses and nurture consciousness to re-equalize closer towards a balanced union: a return to a blissful state of equilibrium and complete trust and submission to Allah SWT.

> **'Know o beloved, that humans were not created**
> **in jest or at random,**
> **but marvelously made and for some great end.'**
> *al-Ghazzali*

The influence of genetics, situational realities and inner/outer senses shape and form mindful awareness: all of our earthly reality is based on the principle of duality, which is inherent in everything, for example, within the meaning of the first pillar of Islam, the 'Shahada', Declaration of Faith or Creed, 'witnessing':

Laa il'laha il'Lallah – there is no god, but GOD – the Unifying Creational Energy-Force responsible for our existence here and of what is beyond our knowledge.

Muhammed ur-Rasul'Lallah – Muhammed is the messenger of GOD -
Saying this immediately separates us humans from any Divinity, establishing the existential reality of duality, which we are 'abd', servant to.

It guides us into the framework of Allah's SWT established and approved way to live, as exemplified and taught by all Prophets (peace and blessings be upon them, pbut), all of them having been divinely chosen carriers of Allah SWT's unified and unchanged message.

Through the Holy Scriptural Message (*Tawrat* - Torah, *Injeel* - Gospel, Qur'an) and by the prophetic examples of living correctly, we have been given knowledge to our purpose in life:

To maintain a constant '*jihaad*' – great effort of an inner struggle - to stay on the 'Siratul-Mustaqeem' - the best, the middle, the straight path and 'encourage to do good and to refrain from evil'.

To find balance (virtue) between extreme polarities (vices) in any given dynamic: generosity (virtue), being between miserliness and indiscriminate wastefulness (vices); precaution (virtue) between anger and indifference (vices) etc.

A famous Hadith relates that,
"man 'arafa nafsahu faqad 'arafa Rabbahu"
"the one who knows his/her self,
has thus come to know his/her Lord."

which tells me, that to understand the 'inner', I need to get to know my*self*, so I can better understand my Creator, The Grand Creational Plan and the reason for my being created.

With knowledge of reality's duality, and intending to be balanced every moment on a virtuous path of appropriate understanding and choice, my next step towards 'inner awakening' may be directed to uncover potential light and truth within...

'the nafs is like a flame,
both in its display of beauty
and its hidden potential for destruction.
Though its color is attractive, it burns.'
Bakharzi

To nurture 'self-knowledge' I need to concentrate on becoming 'abdul waqt – servant of the moment', as with each intake of breath and each breathing out, a new moment is created with possible means of self-discipline and inner spiritual growth.

Each new moment I need to re-direct my awareness towards

dhikr ul'lah – remembering Allah SWT, implementing the Qur'anic Message and the prophetic ways…

In a Hadith Qudsi:

'I (Allah) cannot be contained by heaven and earth, but I can be found within the heart of the believer.'

As we witness the powerful oppositional forces of duality, 'attraction and repulsion' played out throughout a person's life at all times, we come to understand that these dual realities must have tremendous significance and are potential stepping-stones on the path towards self-knowledge.

These forces are in constant interplay, and sometimes one might dominate the other and then vacillate back again; in this way a young child constantly is acquiring knowledge of simple consequences to his/her actions. The relevant question to the care of each person becomes: are these forces more or less balanced out by each other? Are the 'attractive' and energy giving experiences not overcome by the negative, difficult and aggressive 'repulsions'? And how can they become equalized? Imbalance or dis-ease come about, when the body, heart, self and soul are out of equilibrium, and when terrestrial dynamics dominate over the potentially constantly obtainable inner light (*Ruh*), and Truth is covered or veiled.

As one grows into spiritual maturity and these deep energies are being recognized within (sense-ically, intellectually and emotionally), they now can be trusted upon to create one's self-aware and controlled interacting within any given situation. The result will be appropriate, harmonious and relaxed self-control with a balanced reliance on compassion and peacefulness. There will be constant dependence and trust of the availability of Allah's Mercy and Desire for growth in inner wisdom and development towards a stable and tranquil person, by and with the rope of Allah SWT's Guidance, *Insha'Allah* – God Willing.

Chapter 14
Peace is Life-Giving
by Nancy Meyerhofer

Our best decisions are normally made when we are in a peaceful state, in emotional equilibrium. It is most difficult to make a good decision when I am very disturbed or very euphoric. As a Franciscan, I feel a strong invitation to be "an instrument of peace."

And so I listen to a young man's admission that he is an unwed father, witnessing his shame and pain from a non-judgmental stance. We talk. A few nights later I see him carrying his 10-month-old son in public, and he smiles at me.

Again, I listen as a young woman unburdens her confusion and guilt over a same-sex relationship and accompany her as she discerns her psychosexual orientation and its resulting options. She has carried the secret for two years and has felt unable to speak of it. Her tears are tears of relief that she is no longer alone.

Silence often is not golden. When she was 18, a young woman went to see a "spiritist-curer" for a persistent cough. He convinced her that having sex with him was the only cure. For 12 years she has lived in silence and agony, fearful of having AIDS, too poor to pay for a blood test that would free her from the uncertainly one way or another. Together we examine realistic options that will be of help to her; like where to find free and confidential testing. This knowledge, plus speaking of her abuse for the first time, brings a smile to her face...

If persons can't make good decisions when disturbed, neither can nations. Witness the hasty decisions after 9/11—the Patriot Act giving near-dictatorial powers to a president who is not accountable, Guantánamo Bay and Abu Ghraib and so many other abuses of human rights justified by our fear and desire for vengeance. Pope Paul VI stated so well, "If you want peace, work for justice." We need to ask hard questions of ourselves, one of which is, "Are we ready to do what it takes to ensure a true and lasting peace?"

> *There is a hunger within people for peace*
> *(within us, between each other)*
> *and a desire to live from within that center*
> *in our everyday world.*
>
> Words of Wisdom from a Spiritual Amma – Jean Springer

Chapter 15
Walking With Others
On The Path To Healing

By Sister Margie Hosch, OSF

Once upon a time, in the setting of a small living room, I had that moment of a heart to heart connection which plunged me into a cauldron of amazing grace. My mid-life questions of the meaning for my life, my quest of a magic wand to wipe away all anxiety, and my search for a "person" connection that would ground my very soul, came by the way of a most normal, ordinary interaction.

When discussing my plight with another I just began to talk and talk and talk without end. After this went on for some time, my listening companion stood up, came to me and held me for as long as I had taken to empty out my life "stuff" that had been smoldering within me for so long. Then, while still holding me, she prayed me to God. I still carry the graces of that held time both physically and spiritually.

Walking with others on the path to healing requires a listening presence, a big heart to hold all the cares and concerns of another, a willingness to take the time, a capacity for loving others, and a basic grounding in one's faith in an extravagant loving God. Healing evolves within each person. We do much work in a one to one relationship. At times we desire an experience that leads us on a journey with others in healing and deepening our relationships with all creation.

Chapter 16
The Unfolding
of my Journey to Healing
Write Your own Chapter

Your story deserves to be in this book also. This chapter is dedicated to you, the reader, to invite you to honor your story. This chapter is an invitation for you to write your own Insights on the Journey. A few story starter lines are listed to spark your creativity.

What I really want to say about my own journey …

My favorite quote about healing...

What I have learned about healing...

The Journey continues ...

No experience is too short to count.

On Quiet

We may not journey to a physical desert,
But we are invited
into the desert of our hearts.

When we discover that
still, quiet that is within,
We can begin to truly listen and to rest.

Words of Wisdom from a Spiritual Amma
- Jean Springer

Resources Suggested by the Writers

1) Eremos Center for Contemplative Living: www.eremos.org
Eremos offers individuals an opportunity to rest, pray, reflect, share and experience peace. Within Eremos the silence is healing; the sharing is respectful and reflective. jseremos@austin.rr.com
512-531-9594 * 6210 Adel Cove * Austin, Texas 78749

2) Capacitar: www.capacitar.org Capacitar means to "empower." Our vision is to heal ourselves and to heal our world. Using a hands-on popular education approach, we teach simple wellness practices that lead to healing, wholeness and peace in the individual and in the world. Capacitar is committed to communities affected by violence, poverty and trauma, uniting people across borders in solidarity, understanding and reconciliation. Capacitar publishes manuals and workshop resources in English, Spanish and other languages. The manuals and materials reflect years of experience and use with grassroots people in different countries and include their stories, suggestions and reflections.
email: capacitar@capacitar.org

3) The P.E.A.C.E. Initiative: (Putting an End to Abuse through Community Efforts Initiative) is a coalition of 48 agencies, organizations and individuals working collaboratively to end violence in families. The P.E.A.C.E. Initiative offers free training and education to groups wanting to learn more about domestic violence. Activities of the P.E.A.C.E. Initiative include: Education and trainings on domestic violence issues, Coalition Building, Community organizing, Advocacy, Outreach, Systems change, and work with the media, artists, policy makers, survivors, community leaders, etc.
P.E.A.C.E. Initiative 1443 S. St. Mary's San Antonio, Texas 78210
Patricia@thepeaceinitiative.net (210) 533-2729
www.thepeaceinitiative.net

4) The National Domestic Violence Hotline: www.ndvh.org
Help is available to callers 24 hours a day. Hotline advocates are available for domestic violence survivors and anyone calling on their behalf to provide crisis intervention, safety planning, information and referrals. Assistance is available in English and Spanish with access to more than 140 languages through interpreter services. If you or someone you know is frightened about something in a relationship, please call: 1-800-799-SAFE (7233) or TTY 1-800-787-3224

5) **First Aid for Trauma Survivors**: 1-877-Patience
www.patiencepress.com

6) **Dana Clark and Kevin Lewis' Music**: to find out more about Dana's musical mission, go to the website www.danaclarkmusic.com. For information about the music of Dana and her husband Kevin Lewis go to www.lewisandclarkmusic.com

7) **The Peace Choir of San Antonio**: learn the favorite songs of the Peace Choir at: www.cdbaby.com/cd/songsofpeace

8) **The peaceCENTER of San Antonio**: www.salsa.net/peace peaceCENTER eBooks can be purchased at this website. To purchase traditional paperback editions of this and any of the other peaceCENTER books, go to Amazon.com and enter the title of the book in the search box.

9) **Tina Karagulian**: www.tinakaragulian.com
Tina has photos of her art available at this website.

10) **Martha K. Grant**: www.marthakgrant.com
Martha Grant's art features hand-dyed and screenprinted fiber creations.

11) **Sisters of St. Francis**: 563-583-9786 or www.osfdbq.org

12) **The Academy of Self-Knowledge**: www.askonline.co.za. The Academy is an on-line interactive study course developed and overseen by Shaykh Fadhlalla-Haeri, in which he attempts to open for his students, windows towards understanding and knowledge of one's inner and spiritual journey.

13) **The San Antonio Muslim Women's Association** can be reached at samuslimwomen@gmail.com. Narjis Pierre also recommends www.nuradeen.com

14) **Nia Technique, Inc**.: www.nia-nia.com
Nia is a body-mind-spirit fitness and lifestyle practice. Through expressive movement Nia empowers people to achieve physical, mental, emotional and spiritual well-being. 1-800-762-5762.

15) **Camp Courageous**: is a special camp that brings together the fun of a recreational camp with grief support for youth ages 7 - 17. Camp Courageous is offered free of charge to campers. Click under the Families and Community section of www.hopehospice.net or call: 1- 800-532-8192.

16) **Connections**: provides a safe and secure alternative from the "streets" for homeless, abused, or at-risk youth.
Visit www.connectionsnonprofit.org or call the 24 hour crisis hotline at: 1-800-532-8192.

17) **Family Services Association**: is dedicated to helping children, seniors, and families in need. Family Services Association provides high quality service in English and Spanish to clients of all ethnic and racial backgrounds and all socio-economic levels. www.Family-Service.org (210) 299-2400

18) **Women's Global Connection**: is an interactive web site designed to promote the learning and leadership capacity of women around the world. There are opportunities for online discussions, conversations, and other exchanges. www.womensglobalconnection.org

(19) **Wholeness Holiness Retreat**: Women may come to a time in their life when they desire a greater integration of the emotional and spiritual journey. Our hearts search for the living God in the midst of living through the seasons of our lives. Out of this basic desire for an integration of body, mind and spirit, the Wholeness Holiness Retreat was created. This retreat opens the minds and hearts of women to emotional and psychological wholeness by

❖ Addressing the crises and traumas each person has had or is having that are impacting present beliefs, feelings, behaviors, and an identity of self.
❖ Using multiple strategies for helping each woman develop a new sense of inner strength and self nurturing.
❖ Empowering women to make the necessary changes that bring healing and growth for leading more fulfilling lives.

Women come, seeking a greater wholeness in grieving loss, discerning future direction, healing relationships, managing conflict, aging concern, mid-life issues, working through abuse, divorce, family of origin issues of distance or enmeshment, ministry burn out, transitions, dealing with illness, facing death, a time of quiet to commune with God, and search for meaning in a new season of their life.

This once in a lifetime life changing retreat provides for individual attentiveness to each retreatant and for the group members' listening and caring presence. The retreat directors will travel to your location if you can provide the place and up to seven retreatants. You may also make it at one of the retreat places in South Carolina.

Each retreatant has four daily scheduled one hour sessions of: Individual spiritual direction, Individual counseling, Group shared prayer, Group counseling.

The retreat gradually moves each person to an integration of the spiritual and psychological aspects of one's life. Each person leaves in the loving embrace of God and in the loving embrace of the other retreatants and retreat directors. The retreatants will be strengthened to become the eyes, hands, feet, and hearts to their brothers and sisters who will be calling upon them in their need. They will develop "eyes" to see what the other needs. This Intentional Compassion is all about walking with others on the path to healing and wholeness.

For a brochure, schedule of retreats or more information:
phone: 843-902-6807 or 864-483-2648
e-mail: retreat@sccoast.net or hoschm@osfdbq.org

Author Biographies

Maureen Leach, OSF is a Dubuque Franciscan Sister. She is on the core team of the peaceCENTER. She serves as a Spanish/English Interpreter for the Sisters of Charity of the Incarnate Word. She is also a Licensed Massage Therapist. Her mission as a massage therapist is to promote health and healing in the world through massage.

Nancy Olinger owns and manages a ranch east of San Antonio, Texas, where she raises cattle and horses. Her spirit of adventure and creativity knows no bounds, and her mind has the artist's eye for imagination and detail. Her hands create visual stories reflecting her own free spirit. Whatever she creates, paints, or sculpts, one can be sure that it will be an expression that is unique . . . and uniquely Nancy.

Jean Springer is the Spiritual Amma of Eremos Center of Contemplative Life. From the womb her life has been directed by the Spirit. Raised Baptist and living next to the Baptist Church, much of her time was spent within the influence of the church. As a teenager she longed to become a missionary, but it took becoming Catholic and entering a missionary community of women to make the desire a reality. Eight years in South Africa gave her a hunger and thirst for a contemplative way of life. She searched all over the United States for a community which would affirm and support the calling. Lebh Shomea House of Prayer in south Texas honored that search. The 10-year ebb and flow in relationship within that community gave her another desire. Seeing so many people seeking God within silence and solitude, she moved to Austin in 1992 to respond to her longing to provide a space where people could step back from their everyday lives on a more regular basis to listen to the Spirit. She has served as a spiritual Amma at Eremos since its inception.

Polly A. Fowler, a native of Laredo, Texas, has been writing music and poetry since she was 12 years old. A former English teacher and school counselor, she retired from the educational system after 34 years and in 2004 began her current practice as a psychotherapist. For the past 35 years she has been the director of the St. Pius X Folk Choir where many of her musical compositions have been included in liturgical worship. For Polly, her music and her poetry give voice to the soul, so often touched by pain, yet always seeking hope, healing and connections to all that is life-giving.

Catherine Na is a native San Antonian who has served in pastoral ministry and community development. Her poetry springs from her own experiences; she shares it with us in belief with the philosopher that "what is most personal is also the most universal".

Martha K. Grant finds healing in the arts, both visual and written, sometimes combining the two in her hand-dyed and screenprinted fiber creations. www.marthakgrant.com. She was so inspired by the idea of this book on healing that she is planning on writing her own. Watch for it to come out one of these days. She believes that sharing her story may bring healing to others.

Tina Karagulian has twenty years of experience assisting adults, children, and adolescents process life's transitions and gain strength of self through art, play, journaling, meditation and traditional counseling. She walks with clients as they release emotions and limiting beliefs, and then assists them to consciously change those beliefs to ones that empower. As an artist she understands the power of creativity and expression in the healing process. She began drawing as a child and fell in love with the peaceful feelings that came to her while she would draw. As an adult, she has come to honor how art can express deep emotions that have no words. Through her own creative process, Tina has healed losses she has experienced during her life, and also been able to show her joy and passion for living. She often sings spiritual music that uplifts her while she paints, and her intention is to bring that love and peace into each work of art. www.tinakaragulian.com

Naomi Shihab Nye is a Palestinian-American who believes deeply in exchange, dialogue, mutual support, among groups in conflict and also that literature can make a crucial contribution to connection among human beings. Her most recent book is, ***I'll Ask You Three Times, Are You OK? Tales of Driving & Being Driven.*** She has published more than 20 other books of poems, essays, and stories. She has been a visiting writer in hundreds of schools and communities since graduating from Trinity University. Her novel ***Habibi*** has been translated into various languages, including Hebrew, and used in middle schools across the country.

Patricia R. Farrell, OSF, LCSW, is a Franciscan Sister from Dubuque, Iowa, and a licensed clinical social worker. She received a B.A. in English and secondary education from Briar Cliff University in Sioux City, Iowa, and an MSW from Loyola University Chicago. Her special studies in the area of trauma include levels 1 and 2 of EMDR (Eye Movement Desensitization and Reprocessing) and Hakomi Integrative Somatics Training for the Treatment of Trauma. She has been working in cross-cultural settings from 1974 until the present, traveling in Latin America and doing trauma trainings in Guatemala and Colombia. During twenty years she lived in Latin America and experienced first hand both the military dictatorship in Chile and the civil war in El Salvador, which eventually led her to study clinical social work in order to be prepared to work with immigrants and refugees suffering from trauma. Part of her studies included an internship at the Marjorie Kovler Center for the Treatment of Survivors of Torture in Chicago where she also served for three years as a volunteer translator and therapist. Other recent work experiences have been at Latino Counseling Services, a program of the Counseling Center of Lakeview in Chicago, and Capacitar El Salvador where she worked as a therapist and a trainer in multi-cultural wellness education. She currently lives in Omaha, Nebraska and works as a bi-lingual therapist at the Juan Diego Center and at the International Center of the Heartland.

Brenda entered the military after graduating from college and spent 14 years in service (active duty and as a reservist). In 2001 Brenda began her life with a religious congregation of Roman Catholic sisters and is currently waiting to take her final vows in order to become a fully professed sister. She is presently doing cross cultural ministry in a rural setting.

Patricia S. Castillo, L.M.S.W. has been the Executive Director of the The P.E.A.C.E. Initiative since its inception in 1990. She works tirelessly to educate the community on issues of domestic violence. She has received numerous awards for her work including: Recognition from The MA.T.C.H., Program (Mothers and Their Children - Women detained in Jails) of the Bexar County Adult Detention Center for her work with the women inmates from 1984-2004; The Humanitarian Award from The ASERVIC (Association for Spiritual, Ethical, and Religious Values in Counseling) organization for her "commitment, dedication, support and leadership in the cause of justice for all people especially those women, children and men trapped in violent relationships."; The Santa Maria Justice Award to Patricia S. Castillo, L.M.S.W., from the Center for Legal & Social Justice, St. Mary's University Law School; 2005 Inductee into the San Antonio Women's Hall of Fame in the area of Civic Leadership, as well as the Women's Advocate of the Year from the University of Texas at San Antonio-Women's Studies Institute. She works mostly in San Antonio , Texas and has also worked in Acuna, Cancun , Mexico City and Monterrey, Mexico as well as Honduras, Guatemala, Brazil, Russia, China, several states in the U.S, and the Navajo Reservation.

Elizabeth Cummins, OSF is a spiritual director and bereavement counselor in private practice in Phoenix, AZ. Besides hiking in the desert, she enjoys herb gardening, vegetarian cooking and reading. Liz is a member of the Sisters of St. Francis of Dubuque, IA.

Catherine Laraya Cuasay is proud of her Philippine heritage which immersed her in art, dance, music, poetry and theatre through her childhood. Her work as a Licensed Mental Health Counselor and Expressive Therapist has been leavened by experiences with bereavement groups, couples in conflict, children coping with divorce, developmentally delayed adults, formerly battered women, seniors in geriatric rest homes and partial hospitalization programs, homeless women and children, incarcerated adults, runaway teenagers and trauma survivors. She currently lives in San Antonio remaining avidly involved in community ritual and music ministry as well as hosting an array of workshops and retreats. Catherine holds a vital belief in the power of the arts to transcend culture and language barriers and ultimately to transform wounded lives toward healing.

Dana Clark has spent her life creating music. She is a singer-songwriter and music instructor who plays piano, guitar, flutes, mandolin, sax, and other instruments. She works as Music Director at the Unity Church of San Antonio, Texas, and plays in the band 'Lewis and Clark (Musical) Expedition' with her husband, guitarist and bassist Kevin Lewis. To find out about their music, go to www.lewisandclarkmusic.com.

Michelle Balek OSF, or Shell as she likes to be called, is a member of the Dubuque, IA Franciscan Community. Her BA in Sociology/Social Work prepared her well for her many ministries over the years. She was a Peace Corps volunteer in Ecuador, and has served in the IA Department of Social Services; Catholic Charities in TX and IA; as a Pastoral Associate in an urban parish; on the National Staff of Pax Christi USA; and as the North America Region Coordinator for Franciscans International, a Non-Governmental Organization in consultative status with the United Nations. She recently completed her graduate studies at the School for International Training in Brattleboro, VT, earning an MA in Sustainable Development. She currently serves as the Delegations Coordinator for the Foundation for Self-Sufficiency in Central America (FSSCA).

Glee Miller has been a Catholic minister for 30 years, 13 of those, working in an inner city hospital as a chaplain. Her specialty during those years was Perinatal Loss, helping parents deal with the loss of a baby who died too soon. After retirement, she continues to work as a spiritual director, member of the parish RCIA team at St. Brigid Church in San Antonio, Texas and as an adult educator, teaching others how to minister to grieving parents. She is a certified Lay Minister, holds a Master's degree in Theology and has earned a Doctorate of Ministry for her work with grieving parents. Glee is married to a Baptist minister and together they have four children and seven grandchildren.

Narjis Pierre was born in Australia, and given the name Heidi by her parents. At the age of three the family moved to Switzerland, where she completed her formal education and began her professional career in 'special needs' care. At the age of 29 Heidi left Switzerland, friends and family and went traveling in South America; her path took her northwards into the south of Texas and to a Muslim community established in the Hill Country. There, the journey turned inward: Heidi became Narjis and took on the active learning of 'Islam' and stepped on the path towards understanding mind, heart, self and soul, in another word: sufism. She married an american Muslim, and raised three children. She is engaged in the Muslim community (co-founder of SAMWA - San Antonio Muslim Women's Association), as well as being in dialogue with other faith communities in San Antonio. She presently works at a retirement center. Narjis Pierre authored the 'Hajj Journal' which is available from the peaceCenter website. She is on the Board of the peaceCenter.

Nancy Meyerhofer is a Dubuque Franciscan who has served in various missions, eight years in the United States and nearly 30 in Latin America.

Sister Margie Hosch, OSF is a clinical member of the American Association for Marriage and Family Therapy. She co-authored the Wholeness Holiness Retreat with Sister Dorothy Heiderscheit, OSF, who together gave the retreats to their Franciscan Sisters of Dubuque, Iowa. She has teamed with sisters of two religious communities including Sister Connie Fahey in conducting the retreats in South Carolina. Her experience includes providing individual, family and marriage therapy, group therapy, conducting days and weekends of spiritual renewal and giving individual directed retreats.

3061874

Made in the USA